Agriculture, Rural Banking and Micro Finance in India

Agriculture, Rural Banking
and
Micro Finance in India

Edited by

Rais Ahmad

Formerly, Head and Associate Professor,
Department of Agricultural Economics and Business Management,
Aligarh Muslim University (AMU), Aligarh
and
Formerly, Professor, Centre for Management Studies,
Jamia Millia Islamia, New Delhi

New Century Publications
New Delhi, India

NEW CENTURY PUBLICATIONS
4800/24, Bharat Ram Road,
Ansari Road, Daryaganj,
New Delhi – 110 002 (India)

Tel.: 011-2324 7798, 4358 7398, 6539 6605
Fax: 011-4101 7798
E-mail: indiatax@vsnl.com • info@newcenturypublications.com
www.newcenturypublications.com

Editorial office:
LG–7, Aakarshan Bhawan,
4754-57/23, Ansari Road, Daryaganj,
New Delhi – 110 002

Tel.: 011-4356 0919

First Published: **July 2012**

ISBN: **978-81-7708-324-8**

Published by New Century Publications and printed at Salasar Imaging Systems, New Delhi.

Designs: Patch Creative Unit, New Delhi.

PRINTED IN INDIA

Dedicated to

Professor Shad Bano Ahmad (Retired)

Aligarh Muslim University

Foreword

It is immense pleasure for me to write foreword for this book on **Agriculture, Rural Banking and Micro Finance in India** edited by Dr. Rais Ahmad, former Professor in Management Studies, Centre for Management Studies, Jamia Millia Islamia, New Delhi and formerly with the Department of Agricultural Economics and Business Management, Aligarh Muslim University, Aligarh. India is ranked within the world's five largest producers of over 80 percent of agricultural produce items. It is also one of the world's five largest producers of livestock and poultry meat, with one of the fastest growth rates, as of 2011. Though the share of agriculture in GDP is gradually declining due to emergence of IT and other services, still its importance cannot be undermined. In a sense, one can say that agriculture is backbone of the Indian economy and all its stakeholders deserve special care and treatment by regulatory agencies and need specific patronage.

The subject also receives due attention of academicians and professionals in the field. Many reputed institutions of the country, including Indian Institute of Management, Ahmedabad, have dedicated research centers for studies to address the issues facing the agricultural sector and it's financing. Dr. Rais Ahmad has made praiseworthy efforts to fill in this need to a greater extent by editing this book.

The coverage of articles/research papers is wide and extensive. There are cases, empirically tested studies from various parts of India. The coverage includes areas like 'micro finance' and its role in agriculture, 'rural banking', and lending behavior of banks towards the agriculture sector. Efforts have also been made to include papers in the area of financial inclusion, institutional credit in agriculture field and a comparative study of pre- and post-agricultural reforms in India.

The above book is a timely contribution by eminent experts and scholars. I am sure that this book would prove useful to policy makers, professionals, scholars, and academicians.

March, 2012

Professor Javaid Akhtar
Dean, Faculty of Management
Studies and Research,
Aligarh Muslim University, Aligarh

About the Book

Agricultural sector occupies a key position in the Indian economy. It provides employment to about 65 percent of the working population of India. It is but natural that the problems of farmers are addressed with a sense of urgency. Agriculture being a State subject, the bulk of public investment in agriculture takes place at the level of States and the Central Government supports the States as a catalyst.

Being the backbone of the Indian economy, agriculture has all along been treated as a priority sector for the allocation of institutional credit. The low growth rate of agriculture in the past few years has further strengthened the channels of credit flow to this sector.

Micro credit has emerged as a visible credit channel to the poor as their access to conventional credit channels is constrained by the requirement of collateral and high transaction cost. Micro finance is routed through self-help groups (SHGs). Over the years, SHG–Bank Linkage Programme—which includes commercial banks, regional rural banks and co-operative banks—has emerged as the major micro finance programme in the country.

This volume contains 12 well-researched papers, authored by experts in the field of agricultural finance, which provide an in-depth analysis of current state of agricultural/rural finance in India, emergence of micro finance, financial inclusion efforts and related matters.

Editor's Profile

Dr. Rais Ahmad is formerly Head and Associate Professor, Department of Agricultural Economics and Business Management, Aligarh Muslim University (AMU), Aligarh. He is also ex-Professor of the Centre for Management Studies, Jamia Millia Islamia, New Delhi.

He received his M.Com., M.Phil. and Ph.D. degrees from AMU. He has recently completed a major research project on micro finance and self-help groups (SHGs) financed by University Grants Commission (UGC), New Delhi. He has to his credit 8 books and several research papers published in professional journals.

Contents

Contributors

Amrik Singh Sudan	Post-graduate Department of Commerce, University of Jammu, Jammu.
Rohini Gupta Suri	Coordinator, PGDBM, Directorate of Distance Education, University of Jammu, Jammu.
Anu Chadha	Government Degree College for Boys, Kathua, Jammu and Kashmir.
Sakeer E.	Koneeri House, Kaliyattamukku, Moonniyur, Kerala.
Rais Ahmad	Formerly, Professor in Management Studies, JMI, New Delhi, and formerly, Associate Professor, Department of AEBM, Aligarh Muslim University, Aligarh.
Salini K	Faculty Member (Finance), IIPS, Kanattukara, Thrissur.
Anamika Kaushiva	Assistant Professor, Department of Economics, Sahu Ram Swaroop Mahila Mahavidyalaya, Bareilly.
Kumud Chandra Goswami	Associate Professor, Department of Commerce, Dibrugarh University, Assam.
Ranjit Singh	Assistant Professor, Department of Business Administration, Assam University, Silchar, Assam.
Anurag Singh	Assistant Professor, Department of Business Administration, Assam University, Silchar, Assam.
A. N. Tamragundi	Assistant Professor, Post-graduate Department of Commerce, Karnatak University, Dharwad.

S.G. Hundekar Professor, Post-graduate Department of Commerce, Karnatak University, Dharwad.

Ashish K. Makwana Assistant Professor, SMC College of Dairy Science, Anand Agricultural University, Anand.

P. Adi Lakshmi Professor and Head, Department of Business Administration, P.V.P. Siddhartha Institute of Technology, Kanuru, Vijayawada, Andhra Pradesh.

Rajesh C. Jampala Professor and Head, Department of Commerce and Business Administration, P.B. Siddhartha College of Arts and Science, Siddhartha Nagar, Vijayawada, Andhra Pradesh.

Srinivasa Rao Dokku Assistant Professor, P.V.P. Siddhartha Institute of Technology, Kanuru, Vijayawada, Andhra Pradesh.

Editor's Note on the Book

Agriculture in the Indian Economy

Agricultural sector occupies a key position in the Indian economy. It provides employment to about 65 percent of the working population of India. It is but natural that the problems of farmers are addressed with a sense of urgency. Agriculture being a State subject, the bulk of public investment in agriculture takes place at the level of States and the Central Government supports the States as a catalyst.

Agricultural and allied products like cereals (mainly rice), tea, coffee, cashew, spices, tobacco and leather are important items of India's exports and hence foreign exchange earnings. Agriculture is also the source of raw material for agro-based industries including textiles, cigarettes, jute, sugar, paper, processed foodstuffs and *vanaspati*. Moreover, agricultural sector provides market for capital goods (tractors, pump sets and other agricultural machinery), inputs (fertilisers, insecticides), and light consumer goods. The nation has invested huge resources for the development of agriculture under various plans.

The development of the agricultural sector depends, to a large extent, on such core industries as power, petroleum, fertilisers and machine tools. Thus, there is inter-dependence between agriculture and industry. Two major components of agricultural development strategy have been: (a) subsidies on inputs and (b) minimum support price for output.

Although Indian agriculture is way back compared to the levels in developed countries, some notable developments have occurred over the last 65 years. Large areas which suffered from repeated failures of rainfall have received irrigation, new crops have come to occupy a significant position in the country's production and trade, agricultural and the industrial economies now exert a powerful influence on one another. However, problems of rural indebtedness and the exploitative practices of the village moneylenders continue to haunt the farmers.

Rural Finance

Being the backbone of the Indian economy, agriculture has all along been treated as a priority sector for the allocation of institutional credit. The low growth rate of agriculture in the past few years has further strengthened the channels of credit flow to this sector.

Agricultural production in India depends upon millions of small farmers. It is the intensity of their effort and the efficiency of their technique that will help in raising yields per acre. Because of inadequate financial resources and absence of timely credit facilities at reasonable rates, many of the farmers, even though otherwise willing, are unable to go in for improved seeds and manures or to introduce better methods or techniques. It is, therefore, of the utmost importance that the financial requirements of the farmers are adequately met.

Provision of sufficient and timely credit at fair rates of interest has, therefore, to be considered as an integral part of agricultural development. Assistance rendered by way of credit has, however, to be related to specific items of productive work or of essential costs of cultivation. Following guidelines from the RBI, commercial banks are increasingly devoting attention to agricultural sector to meet its credit needs.

Agricultural growth is crucial for alleviating rural poverty. Access to institutional credit to more farmers and appropriate quantity and quality of agricultural credit are crucial for realising the full potential of agriculture as a profitable activity.

The Government has taken many policy initiatives for strengthening farm credit delivery system for providing credit at affordable rates of interest to support the resource requirements of the agricultural sector. The emphasis of these initiatives has been on providing timely and adequate credit support to farmers with particular focus on small and marginal farmers and weaker sections of society to enable them to adopt modern technology and improved agricultural practices for increasing agricultural production and productivity. The policy essentially lays emphasis on augmenting credit flow at the ground level through credit planning, adoption of region specific strategies and rationalization of lending policies and procedures and bringing down the rate of interest on farm loan.

Need for agricultural credit arises because modern farm technology is costly and the personal resources of the farmers are inadequate. Provision of agricultural credit, as an input, is essential for widespread use of improved agricultural methods.

Sources of agricultural credit are grouped into two categories: (a) institutional sources and (b) non-institutional sources. Institutional sources include co-operative societies, commercial banks and other government agencies. Non-institutional sources comprise moneylenders, landlords, relatives etc.

Emergence of Micro Finance

Micro credit has emerged as a visible credit channel to the poor as their access to conventional credit channels is constrained by the requirement of collateral and high transaction cost. Micro finance is routed through self-help groups (SHGs). Over the years, SHG–Bank Linkage Programme—which includes commercial banks, regional rural banks and co-operative banks—has emerged as the major micro finance programme in the country. The focus under SHG-Bank Linkage Programme is largely on those rural poor who have no sustainable access to the formal banking system. The target groups, therefore, broadly comprise small and marginal farmers, agricultural and non-agricultural labourers, artisans and craftsmen and other poor engaged in small businesses like vending, and hawking.

The programme has been providing the rural poor access to the formal banking system and has achieved several milestones in terms of gender sensitisation, empowerment and poverty alleviation. The programme provides thrift linked credit support to the members of SHGs. While the programme directly benefits the members, it also helps banks in reducing their transaction costs as well as risk in delivering small loans.

The programme has now assumed the form of a micro finance movement in many parts of the country and has started making inroads in the resource poor regions of the country as well.

SHG-Bank Linkage Programme was formally launched in the year 1992 as a flagship programme by National Bank for Agriculture and Rural Development (NABARD) and aptly supported by the RBI through its policy support. The objective is to meet the financial needs of the poor by linking SHGs with the formal credit agencies. The programme envisages organisation of the rural poor into SHGs for building their capacities to manage their own finances and then negotiate bank credit on commercial terms. The poor are encouraged to voluntarily come together to save small amounts regularly and extend micro loans among themselves. Once the group attains required maturity of handling larger resources, the bank credit follows.

A self-help group is a group of about 15 to 20 people from a homogenous class who join together to address common issues. They involve voluntary thrift activities on a regular basis, and use of the pooled resource to make interest-bearing loans to the members of the group. In the course of this process, they imbibe the essentials of financial intermediation and also the basics of account keeping. The members also learn to handle resources of size, much beyond their individual capacities. They begin to appreciate the fact that the resources are limited and have a cost.

Once the group is stabilised, and shows mature financial behaviour, which generally takes up to six months, it is considered for linking to banks. Banks are encouraged to provide loans to SHGs in certain multiples of the accumulated savings of the SHGs. Loans are given without any collateral and at interest rates as decided by banks. Banks find it comfortable to lend money to the groups as the members have already achieved some financial discipline through their thrift and internal lending activities. The groups decide the terms and conditions of loan to their own members. The peer pressure in the group ensures timely repayment and becomes social collateral for the bank loans.

I place on record my deep appreciation and gratefulness to the contributors to this volume. Their worthy contributions provide deep insights into the financial needs of the rural people and the current efforts to meet them.

I am highly indebted to Professor Javaid Akhtar, Dean, Faculty of Management Studies and Research and Former Chairman, Department of Business Administration, Aligarh Muslim University, Aligarh who in spite of his busy schedule spared his valuable time for writing foreword for this book.

Finally, I am highly thankful to Mr. Sandeep Sury, Managing Director, New Century Publications, New Delhi for the cooperation and help extended by him in publication of this book.

May 2012 **Rais Ahmad**
Aligarh

1

Assessing Financial Services in Rural Areas

Amrik Singh Sudan, Rohini Gupta Suri and Anu Chadha

Introduction

Despite more than 30 years of large financial investments and technical assistance programmes, access to financial services in rural areas have not expanded as expected. Recently, donors, academics and Government policy makers have shown renewed interest in rural finance, hoping to build on lessons learned about subsidized interest rates and directed credit. The resurgence of interest can be attributed to the successes of a number of Rural Financial Institutions (RFIs). With assistance from the donor community, they have achieved significant expansion in outreach with financial sustainability (Morduch and Armendariz). In addition, sustainable microfinance, which has emerged and developed in mostly urban and pre-urban settings has applications and lessons for rural finance.

Development experience has shown that deeper, more efficient financial market can contribute to accelerated agriculture growth and greater food security. Scaling up access to a wider array of financial services in rural markets through a range of financial intermediaries becomes critical to help rural households to smooth consumption and enhance labour productivity. Labour is the most important production factor that the poor can contribute. Also, agriculture has strong forward and backward multiplier effects for the overall economy. Economic growth in agriculture is a key pre condition for overall economic growth and poverty reduction.

At present most of the world's poor still live in rural areas (Zeller 2003; Robinson 2001).

The World Bank has renewed its efforts to improve the state of rural financial markets as noted in the 2003 document, "Reaching the Rural poor: A Renewed strategy for Rural Development". The strategy calls for a diversity of products and institutions to meet the financial service needs of rural communities to increase incomes and jobs measurably. This initiative responds directly to recent demands from client countries seeking to build a new rural finance approach modelled upon the successes achieved by the largely urban micro-finance institutions and the achievements of a select number of large Rural Financial Institutions (RFIs).

To help identify new directions for the World Bank's work in rural finance this economic and sector work examines how access to financial services in rural markets in expanded through strategic alliances between financial intermediaries and other commercial and developmental institutions. Strategic alliances are defined broadly as collaborative arrangements between two or more institutions that pool their resources to achieve mutually compatible goals that each institution cannot achieve alone. Such alliances contribute to improving access to financial services in rural markets, by taking advantage of the strengths of the different types of institutions.

Global experience indicates that a number of Rural Financial Institutions (RFIs) have leveraged relationships with other organizations to achieve one or several objectives. These objectives generally fall into the same five categories of objectives found in business world strategic alliances: (i) expands outreach and market service areas, (ii) reduce and manage transaction costs, (iii) broaden clients' access to varied financial products, (iv) acquire new skills for management and staff, and (v) access additional technical and financial resources to achieve or enhance sustainability. At one end of the spectrum of relationships, some are development partnerships while, at the opposite end, others are strategic alliances.

Bhartiya Samruddhi Investments and consulting Service Ltd. (BASIX) is one of India's largest rural/microfinance institutions with a borrowing-client base of 60,000 in 9 States of India, offering a growing range of financial services to its rural client basis. BASIX provide saving deposits, crop loan and credit for non-form activities the group's Krishna Bhima Samruddhi Local Area Bank (KBSLAB), a licensed microfinance bank. None of the operating units within the Bhartiya Samruddhi Investments and consulting Service Ltd. (BASIX) Group have the legal capacity or the organizational capability to provide a variety of non-bank financial services (primarily insurance and risk mitigation/management products) to the client base. Moreover, without these capabilities Bhartiya Samruddhi Investments and consulting Service Ltd. (BASIX) would be hard pressed to install and adopt appropriate loan portfolio risk protection mechanisms and thereby avoid costly financial reversals.

More than a billion poor people lack access to the basic financial services which are essential for them to manage their precarious lives. Good management of even the smallest assets can be crucial to very poor people, who live in precarious conditions, threatened by lack of income, shelter and food. To overcome poverty, they need to be able to borrow, save and invest and to protect their families against risk. But, with little income or collateral, poor people are seldom able to obtain loans from banks and other formal financial institutions. And even when they do have income or collateral, the amounts they require are often too small to appeal to banks.

Microfinance is one way of fighting poverty in rural areas where most of the world's poorest people live. It puts credit, savings insurance and other basic financial services within the reach of poor people. Through microfinance institutions such as credit unions and some non-governmental organizations, poor people can obtain small loans, receive remittances from relatives working abroad and safeguard their savings. Accessing small amounts of credit at reasonable interest rates gives people with the willingness and know how on opportunity to set up a small business. Records show that poor people are a good risk, with higher repayment rates than conventional borrowers. In countries as diverse as Bangladesh, Benin and Dominica, repayment rates are as high as 97 percent.

Poor women often have the best credit ratings. In Bangladesh, for example, women default on loans less than men, and credit extended to women has a much greater impact on household consumption and quality of life for children. Women's status both in their homes and communities, is improved when they are responsible for loans and for managing savings. When they generate and control their own income, women gain a level of power that means they can make decisions independently and command more respect.

Rural Finance: Cracking the Nut

Access to financial services is an important piece of the complex puzzle of rural development. The benefits of financial on household-asset building, consumption smoothing, and risk management-are even more heightened in the rural context. However, rural areas, marked by dispersed populations and limited infrastructure, pose enormous challenges to financial service providers trying to reach different segments of the rural population, and it remains an underserved market.

A recent conference in Washington, D.C., attempted to crack the nut of rural finance. We were particularly inspired by the opening remarks of Chandula Abeywickrama from the Hatton Nation Bank (HNB) of Sri Lanka. HNB is a well established commercial bank that was forced to embark on rural and agricultural finance in the mid-1970s when the government restricted private commercial banks to open branches in urban cities. The bank's approach to rural and agricultural finance provides lessons that can no doubt be useful to all types of financial service providers around the world.

Clear Vision: Seventy percent of the Sri Lankan Population lives in rural areas and is directly and indirectly involved in agriculture. By the late 1980s, HNB saw a great potential with a large underserved rural market, and developed a strategy accordingly. They downscaled part of their regular operations by establishing a dedicated division for microfinance and rural banking to provide not only a wide range of financial products and services, but also extension services (e.g. technical assistance, marketing arrangements). In addition, they went rural with a long term vision, understanding the risks but also acknowledging the long-term rewards.

Delivery Channels: To support its new rural and agricultural finance strategy, HNB invested in new delivery channels to reach rural customers more effectively. New channels included full-fledged customer centres, microfinance units, ATMs, and mobile vehicles. But the bank did not stop with the physical and technical infrastructure, it also invested in developing a large network of field officers.

Right People, Right Place: The bank heavily invested in its human resources by hiring qualified people that not only understood finance, but also had expertise in agriculture. Even the board includes champions of agriculture finance. HNB created a network of 250 'barefoot bankers' who work in the villages and usually come from the community. They act as field officers and also mentor, guide, and provide technical assistance to clients.

Partnerships: HNB established strong relationships with the Central Bank, other government entities, and funders. They worked together to identify opportunities for expansion of rural and agricultural development. In addition, HNB initiated corporate partnerships to make the link between the private agribusiness sector and smallholder farmers. Private agribusiness firms work with farmers to provide them with inputs, technical assistance, assist in agro technologies, and implement buy-back agreements.

Risk Management: HNB is taking risk management seriously, and put several systems in place to mitigate them. At the field level, having the 'barefoot bankers' close to the clients and bringing technical expertise and guidance helped reduce risks. Farmers are encouraged and guided to become commercially viable. In addition, the arrangements between HNB and its corporate partners are designed so that risks are shared or transferred. This resulted in mitigated production risks and market risks.

In short, to crack the nut and have successful rural finance, it is important to take into consideration the unique features of rural markets, customer demand and business requirements, and financial market realities on the ground. What is needed to get rural finance right it quite similar to what is needed to get microfinance more generally right-but perhaps with an extra dose of everything as the context is often more challenging. Major investments in institutional capacity, for example, are required as capacity across the board (financial institutions, end-client, and government institutions) tends to be weaker in rural areas. And when it cones to agricultural finance specifically, addressing the non-financial constraints (quality of inputs, marketing, etc), is key as is collaboration with the government and private sector.

Rural Finance Policy of International Fund for Agricultural Development (IFAD)

The updated IFAD Rural Finance Policy (RFP) was approved by the IFAD Executive Board in 2009. It is aligned with changes in IFAD operating modalities that have occurred since the inception of the Rural Finance Policy (RFP) in 2000 and addresses the specific recommendations made in the agreement at completion point of the corporate-level evaluation of the earlier Rural Finance Policy (RFP).

The updated Rural Finance Policy (RFP) provides guidelines to IFAD decision makers, consultants and partner organizations to ensure the development of a coherent and effective rural finance sector. These guidelines are intended to build clients' skills to effectively participate in the ownership and oversight of local financial institutions; promote financial literacy training; and support protective arrangements for savers, borrowers and lending institutions.

The Rural Finance Policy (RFP) emphasizes the importance of strengthening financial service providers in rural areas, helping savings-based models of community-managed loan funds achieve promising results, and avoiding distortion of financial markets. The updated Rural Finance Policy (RFP) also clarifies IFAD approach to interest rate subsides, credit lines to retail and wholesale finance institutions, and professionally managed credit guarantees.

Building on IFAD experience in rural finance and the good practices developed over time within the sector, six guiding principles are at the core of IFAD approach and support to rural finance. Throughout its interventions in rural finance, IFAD works to:

1. Support access to a variety of financial services, including savings, credit, remittances and insurance.
2. Promote a wide range o financial institutions, models and delivery channels.
3. Support demand-driven and innovative approaches.
4. Encourage-in collaboration with private sector-partners-market-based approaches that strengthen rural financial markets, avoid distortions in the financial sector and leverage IFAD resources.
5. Develop and support long-term strategies focusing on sustainability and poverty outreach.
6. Participate in policy dialogues that promote an enabling environment for rural finance.

IFAD: Decision Tools for Rural Finance

IFAD Decision Tools for Rural Finance are designed to provide decision-making support for country programme (CPMs), consultants, project staff and technical advisers who develop and implement rural finance projects.

However, on the IFAD Rural Finance Policy (REP) (IFAD 2009), as well as other good practice guides, this knowledge management tool is designed to help identify and answer the questions that arise in each rural finance project, provide background on key issues, define common terms, highlight risks and opportunities, and provide references for further investigation.

The Decision Tools are divided into five main sections, each with a specific objective:

1. **Understanding the Fundamentals:** Review rural finance basics and IFAD role in the sector.
2. **Assessing the Market:** Analyse the status of a financial sector and identify the gaps.
3. **Designing a Project:** Define the interventions in a rural finance project.
4. **Assessing and Selecting Project Implementation Partners:** Assess and select project implementation partners through a transparent competitive process.
5. **Conducting Performance Monitoring and Evaluations:** Effectively conduct ongoing and annual performance monitoring.

This operational tool is the result of an intensive consultation process with colleagues both within outside IFAD. The Decision Tools were discussed and reviewed with IFAD Thematic Group on Rural Finance and with key leaders from numerous partner institutions and centres of excellence in microfinance.

The Decision Tools are a 'living document' that will be continuously updated and improved to reflect the development of the industry, innovations, IFAD increasing experience and case studies of these good practices at work.

Constraints to Accessing Financial Services in Rural Areas

Rural financial markets in developing countries face several critical constraints that limit the availability of financing for both agricultural and off-farm activities. In some cases, the menu of financial services is limited to short term credit. In other cases there are significant geographical gaps where no formal financial intermediaries are present. Thus, the growth of rural markets is often impeded by a scarcity of viable financial institutions and by a limited range and lack of affordability of financial services available. Even when short-tern working capital credit is available, rural communities may not have reliable access to savings services, long-term working capital credit is available, rural communities may not have reliable access to savings services, long-term financing for equipment, payments and money transfer services, or insurance products (Rutherford, Matin, and Hulme 1999).

The main constraints to the sustainable provision of financial services in rural markets include the following:

1. Low levels of economic activity and population density result in dispersed demand for financial services, leading to high information collection and transaction costs which make rural clients less attractive for market-driven financial institutions.
2. Weak institutional capacity of community-based rural finance providers, limit the potential for cost-effective alliances with commercial financial institutions.
3. Limited capital resources for credit and ability to provide non-credit services such as savings, check clearing, payments and money transfers curtail rural finance providers from scaling up access to finance in rural markets.
4. Problems with registry systems for land title and moveable assets limit acceptable collateral that rural producers may be able to provide.
5. Seasonality and co-variance of agricultural and farm production activities, which lower likely margins and increase the risks of such operations.

Despite the importance of these constraints, in every region there are MFIs that have overcome the costs and other challenges of extending access into rural markets. The next section analyzes the range of microfinance providers which have overcome these barriers.

Leaders in Rural Financial Market Access

Success in large scale rural finance outreach comes in different institutional forms, especially through a new breed of agricultural development banks, postal financial networks, specialized microfinance institutions (NGO MFIs; regional, development and rural banks; non-bank finance companies; and other legal forms) and credit unions/cooperative financial institutions. Input-supply contracts between rural producers and suppliers, and output-marketing linkages between rural producers and distributors have also expanded access to finance in rural areas.

Similarly, access is being expanded through better knowledge and dissemination about a number of financial instruments such as warehouse receipts and lease financing mechanisms. On the other hand, commercial banks do not generally seem to fit this market niche, although there are some notable exceptions. Some NGO MFIs have tried to transform into regulated, supervised financial institutions but this has not always resulted in expanded financial services and outreach in rural areas.

Agricultural development banks in a few countries have succeeded in progressing into more sustainable institutions by offering demand-driven financial services, building credible lending contracts and using full-cost recovery interest rates. Dynamic and profitable leaders in Asia include Thailand's Bank for Agriculture and Agricultural cooperatives (BAAC), Bank Rakyat Indonesia's (BRI) village units in its micro-banking system (Zeeler 2003; Yaron and Charitonekno 1999), and the privatization and restructuring of Mongolia's Agricultural Bank (Boomgard, Boyer, and Dyer 2003). In East Africa, Tanzania's National Microfinance Bank also demonstrates that state-owned banks can be transformed into successful rural financial intermediaries with business oriented reforms. However, this can only be achieved when there is firm political commitment, ownership of reforms, management autonomy and incentives (Zeller 2003).

Formal and Informal Financial Services

Rural finance is about providing financial services-secure savings, credit, money transfer and insurance in rural areas. Indeed, financial services can play an important role in rural development:

1. Saving and insurance schemes assist the rural population in reducing vulnerability to risks, planning more reliably for the future and saving for upcoming investments, as well as smoothing out irregular income flows and covering unexpected expenses. The latter is particularly important in rural areas where income depends on agricultural cycles.
2. Loans for investments and working capital are crucial elements that enable rural entrepreneurs to make investments, seize economic opportunities and purchase agricultural inputs and working capital. Short-term consumption or emergency loans can help households to avoid difficult situations that might have forced them to sell an asset. However, loans are not always favourable: some poor borrowers experience difficulties in repaying their debts, due either to circumstances beyond their control (e.g. sickness, theft, natural disasters) or to a lack of knowledge and wrong investment strategies.
3. Money transfer services make it possible for people who leave rural areas to work in cities or abroad to send home their remittances safely and at reasonable costs.
4. In addition to fostering rural development, rural finance is increasingly used as an incentive to promote sustainable use to natural resources, use of alternative energies, and environmentally sound behaviour. In recent years, several banks and microfinance institutions have attempted to

achieve not only financial and social, but also environmental sustainability, which has been dubbed the "triple bottom line".

5. Despite the significant demand for financial services in rural areas, institutions offering financial services-such as banks, credit unions, microfinance institutions (MFI) or insurance companies–are typically reluctant to serve rural areas. As a result, the majority of the developing world's rural population does not have access to the formal financial system. Confronted with this lack of access, households, farmers and small entrepreneurs rely on informal ways of accessing financial services.
6. Lending among relatives, neighbours and friends: entrepreneurs usually rely on family or borrow money from friends to make small investments, and in emergency situations people tend to borrow from acquaintances. Such loans are usually repaid without interest.
7. Moneylenders and pawnbrokers: in the absence of formal institutions people typically rely on moneylenders to obtain loans. Moneylenders often ask for usurious interest rates and sometimes try to recover the loans by violent means. On the other hand, moneylenders can provide loans rapidly in an emergency and they do not ask for collateral.
8. Community self-help schemes: such as self-help groups (SHG), rotating savings and credit associations (ROSCAs), community-based savings and credit mechanisms are useful instruments to encourage savings, provide small-scale insurance and avoid debt at exorbitant interest rates.
9. In the absence of banks and official money transfer agents, money transfer is frequently carried out by bus drivers or small shops collaborating with a network of migrants abroad. These services are cheaper than official money transfer providers, but they are not always as secure and reliable.

While the existence of informal services highlights the

general demand for financial services, informal services are usually not sufficient to seize economic opportunities in rural areas to the full. Family and group saving are often too small to pay for important investments. Moreover, they are not always available in cases of emergency. This is particularly true for emergencies caused by natural disasters: if the whole region is affected, no neighbour will be able to help out. Furthermore, most loans from moneylenders are too expensive to be profitable, and debt can lead to dependency of borrowers on moneylenders.

Formal institutions can offer a broader range of financial products. Formal services such as microfinance cannot replace loans from friends and family, but they do complement them and enable the rural population to access a wider range of services. Moreover, formal financial institutions belong to the economic infrastructure of a country or region and can thus help to foster economic development.

Challenges of Rural Finance

Many obstacles still make it difficult for rural households and entrepreneurs to access financial services. Accordingly, both service users and financial institutions offering services in rural areas are confronted with a broad array of challenges:

1. **High Transaction Costs:** Provision of financial services in rural areas is associated with high unit costs both for institutions and for their clients. This is due to the fact that infrastructure for transport, communication and information technology is less developed in rural areas, as well as to the remoteness of these areas. Clients frequently have to travel long distances to deposit savings or repay a loan. As they usually travel on foot, this can cost them an entire working day. Rural financial institutions face additional costs for ensuring security and managing liquidity. High unit costs are usually passed on to the clients, with the result that users in rural areas frequently pay higher interest rates than people in urban areas.

2. **Higher Risks:** Credit risk is higher in rural areas both for borrowers and for rural financial institutions. The revenues of rural households, whose incomes mostly depend on seasonal agricultural and livestock production, are volatile due to fluctuating weather conditions and pests or diseases. In addition, price fluctuations are high in the agricultural sector. Generally, rural households depend on one or two sources of income only, increasing the risk of credit default. Many households either entirely lack collateral or do not have a legal title to their house or land. Financial institutions thus have no means of securing their credits against defaulting. Defaulting clients run high risk as well: financial institutions will typically impose punitive interest rates for delayed payments and might even confiscate assets of defaulting clients.
3. **Higher Rates of Illiteracy:** In developing countries illiteracy rates are particularly high in rural areas. Poorly educated people face an additional challenge in accessing financial services: it is difficult for them to analyse credit risks and the profitability of a loan or savings scheme, to provide all documents and information (such as a business plan) required to apply for a loan, and to understand conditions and contracts. Some institutions fail to communicate interest rates and commissions in a transparent manner, and small prints in contracts can contain additional costs for borrowers. On the other hand, financial institutions that wish to expand into rural areas experience difficulties in finding, hiring and keeping well trained staff that is willing to work in a rural region. Lack of experienced staff, in turn, leads to poor institutions capacity among rural financial institutions.
4. **Addressing the Difficulties:** Promotion of rural finance remains a priority of many governments, donors and Non Governmental Organisations (NGOs), since several challenges still need to be addressed. Rural finance can be promoted by supporting informal schemes such as

community-based savings groups, as well as by fostering formal institutions through technical assistance (supply-side measures) and assisting poor households and small enterprises in accessing financial services (demand-side measures). In addition, donors can support the development of favourable policy and regulatory frameworks.

Various approaches have been developed over the last decades to address the challenges of rural finance. In the 1970s and 1980s, governments channelled subsidized credits through centrally managed development banks; Non-Governmental Organisations (NGOs) and development projects promoted access to credit through so called revolving funds. The objective of these initiatives was to increase the availability of funds for rural and, in particular, agricultural credit. None of these approaches turned out to be financially sustainable, and the majority of the rural population remained excluded from access to financial services.

In the mid-1980s, a shift occurred towards a more demand-oriented approach, with the aim of building inclusive and sustainable financial systems. This approach takes the demand of farmers and rural entrepreneurs for savings, loans and insurance as an entry point. Indeed, when institutions offer financial products tailored to the needs of the rural population, low-income households do use saving schemes, are willing and able to pay interest rates, and buy insurance to cover their risks. Moreover, experience has shown that financial institutions only increase their outreach–to rural areas, but also to poorer clients–if they can cover their costs. Several financial institutions (such as Bank Rakyat in Indonesia, BAAC in Thailand, and FDL in Nicaragua) have demonstrated that it is possible to operate in rural areas and be financially sustainable.

5. **Need Orientation:** Rural households and small

entrepreneurs have specific needs which may vary from those of urban clients. An institution thus has to offer a variety of financial products and flexible services that are adapted to rural clients. For instance, in rural areas most households depend on agricultural cycles. Monthly or even weekly deposits for loan repayment and savings accumulation, as they are promoted by urban microfinance institutions, are simply not tailored to the needs of rural clients. It is therefore important that financial institutions understand the cash flow of rural households and offer adapted loan repayment and savings collection schemes. For example, such a scheme can involve monthly interest rate payments, while the capital is paid back in two or three instalments after the harvest.

6. **Innovation:** Financial institutions need to be innovative to reduce costs. Innovations distribution channels such as mobile branch offices or banking counters located in rural post offices and shops can help to reduce the fixed costs of an institution. Moreover, the use of information technology such as handheld computers or mobile phones is a helpful way of cutting transaction costs. A reduction in costs can improve access to financial services for rural borrowers and savers, as well as leading to a reduction in interest rate and transaction costs.
7. **Minimizing Risks:** While financial institutions in rural areas often lack collateral or the possibility to legally enforce contracts, they can use social links (for example, through group savings and leading) to reduce their risks. The so-called linkage model combines informal systems such self-help group with formal banks. Groups are linked to the bank through a group contract, so the bank does not have to deal with each client separately. This way the bank or microfinance institution can reduce its risks and transfer costs to the self-help group.
8. **Building on Existing Institutions:** Wherever possible, promoters of rural finance should build on existing

institutions rather than create new ones. One way of doing this is to provide commercial banks with technical assistance to extend their services into rural areas (so-called "downscaling"). Furthermore, donors can support existing institutions in reducing costs and, thus, interest rates by helping them to develop more efficient distribution mechanisms and new products and to increase their efficiency through training, but also by assisting poor households and small enterprises in accessing financial services.

Unfortunately, even if financial institutions offer their services at reasonable costs, interest rates for loans remain high in rural areas. There is generally little or no competition among financial institutions in rural areas, and, consequently, the pressure to reduce interest rates is low. Competition needs to be fostered by attracting more financial institutions to rural areas. This, in turn, requires a favourable legal, economic and potential environment.

A precondition for the development of rural financial systems is a stable political and macro-economic environment. Uncertainty about the future political situation of a country and its economic development, particularly inflation, are unfavourable conditions for investments. Moreover, policymakers should give clear signals in favour of rural development, especially the development of inclusive financial institutions in rural areas.

Improved road infrastructure, telecommunication possibilities and security in rural areas are essential in reducing transaction costs of financial services in rural areas, but also in promoting trade linkages between rural and urban regions and in attracting other economic actors.

Rural areas generally lack legal environments enabling a sound development of the financial system and the economy. In more concrete terms, land tenure and property rights are frequently unclear, the administration is slow and inefficient, law enforcement is costly and slow, and the court system lacks transparency and efficiency. Any measures to improve these aspects will help to promote rural financial systems.

Every country regulates its formal financial sector through state laws and regulations. In order to accommodate a well-functioning financial sector, a country's legal and regulatory framework should be clear and transparent, promote competition among institutions, and be favourable for the development of financial services for those persons who have been traditionally excluded of financial services for those persons who have been traditionally excluded from the formal banking sector.

Given the particular difficulties of financial institutions operating in rural areas, laws and regulations should be designed to foster the development of rural financial institutions. While regulations are certainly necessary, overly strict regulations can also become a disincentive for institutions interested in expanding into rural areas. For example, in many countries regulations require financial institutions serving the agricultural sector to accumulate higher regulatory liquidity reserves, both because these institutions face higher portfolio risks and because their clients have no hard collateral. This discourages financial institutions from lending to the agricultural sector. In addition, when regulations are too strict, informal microfinance providers (such as NGOs) have difficulties to obtain a formal status, and, in some cases, become illegal and have to cease operating.

An experience that has been made over and over again is that legal interest rate ceilings are not an appropriate measure to fight against high costs for clients. On the contrary, it has proven to be essential for financial institutions aiming to become financially self-sustainable to charge fees that cover their costs-and these costs are higher in rural areas. Where regulations prevent financial institutions from charging sufficient interest rates to cover their costs, these fees are collected by other means, such as administrative fees and required savings. These often remain in transparent for the clients-who end up paying a lower interest rate, but much higher fees. Alternatively, financial institutions that are not able to cover their costs refrain altogether from offering their services in rural areas.

Agricultural Production and Financial Services

An overwhelming majority of the rural population in developing countries depends on agriculture for survival. Rural financial institutions thus often provide services for activities related to agriculture, such as input supply, production, or distribution and marketing of agricultural products. As pointed out above, providing financial services to the agricultural sector involves specific challenges related to sector-specific risks and to other specific characteristics of agricultural activities, such as seasonality and long maturation processes. Loans for agricultural production or livestock breeding usually have longer terms than those for trade or small industry.

In addition, rural households need financial services that are adapted to the agricultural cycle, such as savings schemes to provide cash for the season in between harvests, or transfer schemes for remittances for migrants who leave the rural areas for seasonal work. There is also a need for agricultural insurance schemes among small farmers who have to protect themselves against weather-related risks. Providing affordable insurance to small farmers remains a challenge due to the pooled risks involved (natural disasters causing damage to many clients at once). Institutions providing such insurance schemes need to be reined by big international insurance companies in order to spread the risk beyond their geographic region. An intermediate solution for insurance scheme is to offer safe and accessible savings and deposit services.

Even though profitability in agriculture is generally low and interest rates are high, it is possible for rural financial institutions to operate on a cost-covering basis and offer financial services to farmers. The following examples will provide some insight into how development projects can support better collaboration between clients and institutions in order to increase access to financial services.

Credit for Horticultural Producers in Kosovo

Commercial banks in Kosovo have shown impressive growth rates since the 1999 conflict. Yet by 2006, only 2 percent of their portfolio was allocated to agriculture—even though the agricultural sector is widely considered as having the greatest potential to generate income and employment. Credit products had not been designed to meet the specific requirement of agriculture, and banks considered lending for agriculture as risky.

A project for horticultural promotion in Kosovo has supported reestablishment of the apple industry with an emphasis on promoting the development of small and medium-scale orchards. To address one of the most important problems faced by small farmers—namely lacking access to banking services—the project collaborated with a major commercial bank. The bank established a specific credit product for orchard investments which involved a loan period of five years and an 18 months grace period.

The project, in turn, contributed to reducing the bank's perceived risk by providing a generic business plan based on the latest technical and market information and agreeing to carry out the first vetting of applicants based on technical criteria. The bank subsequently established a pilot credit line of 100,000 Euros on the requested terms. While many medium and larger farmers seized the opportunity of accessing a loan to establish apple orchards, only five small producers applied for loans. Other small farmers reported the 14 percent interest rate to be too high.

The bank, however, remains committed to expanding its agriculture portfolio-including credits for planting apple orchards. The project, on its part, has continued to work on reducing the perceived risk of investing in small horticultural producers. Soon, it will be able to present members of the

Bankers' Association of Kosovo with software enabling credit officers and business advisers to develop tailor-made credit plans for horticultural investments for individual producers based on the latest technical and market information.

Financial Services for Farmers in Madagascar

In Madagascar, a programme called SAHA provides several forms of support for Central Farmers' Organizations (CFOs), which are made up of several village associations, in order to improve their access to financial services. In particular, the programme facilitates the relations between Central Farmers' Organizations (CFOs) and microfinance institutions.

In the District of Miandrivazo, a mutual microfinance institution was forced to close down after 7 years of activity due to liquidity problems. Following an analysis of the need for financial services among Central Farmers' Organizations (CFOs) members, SAHA launched a lobbying campaign among other microfinance institutions ion Madagascar to explore possible ways of collaboration and accelerate the installation of at least one of them in Miandrivaso.

SAHA also provides targeted support in institutional development to microfinance institutions that have a potential for becoming long-term financial service providers. For example, the programme assists a microfinance institution call TITEM in transforming its legal status, elaborating a business plan, and in its financial management. SAHA also collaborates with farmers to improve their demands.

The programme raises awareness among its partners, provides information about the conditions of access to credit and savings services, and conveys basic knowledge of the functioning of financial markets and household financial management.

Working with the Livestock Value Chain in Mali

In Mali, livestock production contributes 10 percent of the

Gross Productive Product (GDP). Nevertheless, the majority of livestock breeders have great difficulties accessing credit despite the existence of numerous banks and a relatively well developed microfinance sector. A study by the Jekasy programme explored the financing problems experienced by the actors of the livestock value chain in 2007. The study revealed that although livestock producers' cooperatives are eligible to credit from financial institutions, they have trouble accessing credits due to issues of guarantee. Indeed, financial institutions seem reluctant to accept herds as collateral for bank loans. Following this study, Jekasy contributed to developing services for livestock producers' organizations, such as support and consulting with regard to project and business plan elaboration, negotiating with financial institutions to access their products, and implementation of business projects.

Financial Services for Product Processing and Market Access

The development of rural areas depends on access to markets, be it local, national or export markets. Different actors along the value chain, from the input provider to the producer to the consumer-cultivators, processors, traders, wholesalers, retailers-depend on access to financial services to better carry out their economic activities.

Financial institutions that target the development of a given agricultural value chain should have detailed knowledge of the actors and mechanisms in this value chain and offer well adapted services. The following example describes some instruments and financial products that can be used to improve access to financial services for several actors along a value chain.

Support of Value Chains: The Case of Quinoa in Bolivia

The cultivation of quinoa has become increasingly important in the Bolivian highlands ever since the early nineties. While the value chain of quinoa was on the rise, access to financial services adapted to the specific and characteristic demands of the different value chain actors was not granted. This is why in 2005, the Autapo and PROFIN foundations set up a programme to provide value chain actors with financial products that met their needs. Building on five existing microfinance institutions that were already linked to the quinoa sector, the portfolio disbursed to this sector could be increased from US$ 91,000 to currently US$ 3,000,000.

The microfinance institutions expanded their range of products in two ways: on the one hand, they adapted the existing traditional financial products such as individual credit to the specific demands of the quinoa value chain, and on the other hand they introduced new, innovative products such as micro-leasing (ownership of equipment remains with the microfinance institution until the last instalment is paid by the client), micro-warrant (guarantee based on product stored, in order to obtain good price for the quinoa), risk capital, and seed capital. While the programme is still running, highly interesting new products such as agricultural insurance are being developed.

Conclusion

Although the importance of financial services for rural development has been recognized for several decades and the microfinance boom in recent years has once more underlined the importance of financial services, large parts of the world's rural population remain excluded from formal financial services. This mismatch of demand and offer can be explained, first of all, by the challenges faced by rural financial institutions—namely a difficult legal and economic environment, high transaction costs, and higher risks in agricultural lending. Secondly, financial products offered are not always demand-oriented, and institutions do not invest enough in careful product design. Agricultural credit has to be available over long terms, and repayment schemes should be adapted to the agricultural cycle.

Particularly the poorest parts of the rural population are excluded from access to financial services. Experience has show that it is difficult to reach the poorest by focusing on credit only. Poor households need means to reduce their vulnerability. Therefore, the emphasis should be placed more on savings and insurance services, rather than on credit only. Development of affordable and functioning insurance schemes is particularly important, and will increasingly become so.

Despite these challenges there are many positive examples of increased access to financial services in rural areas. Lessons learnt in the past should guide donors in continuing to promote rural finance: by supporting farmers and households in accessing services, by assisting institutions in offering adapted products at a reasonable price, and by promoting an improved regulatory framework. However, the promotion of access to financial services should always be seen as one piece in the larger puzzle of rural development: work towards a sustainable social and economic development of rural areas must include many other aspects, as well.

Rural finance will certainly remain on the agenda of governments and development agencies in the years to come, as larger parts of the population remain excluded from the formal financial system. To tackle this issue, governments might increasingly collaborate with the private sector to find innovative solutions. Moreover, the ongoing integration of many rural areas into regional and even global markets will lead towards an improved infrastructure, which will also include financial institutions. At the same time, these changes will also expose parts of the population to the risk of becoming even more vulnerable and losing their livelihood. These are the people who should be enabled to adapt to such changes with the help of savings and affordable insurance.

References

Adams, Dale W.; Graham, Douglas H.; Von Pischke, John D. 1984, "Undermining Rural Development with Cheap Credit".

Adams, Richard H., Jr. 2004. "Remittances and Poverty in Guatemala." World Bank Research Group Policy Research Paper, June 25 Draft.

BASIX (Bhartiya Samruddhi Investments and Consulting Services Ltd., India), "BASIX: An Overview, "http://www.basixindia.com/overview.htm.

Bucaro, Edgar R. 2001. "The Case of Genesis Empresarial, Guatemala: Poverty Reduction Programs and Rural Development-Impact, Sustainability and Lessons Learned."

Buchenau, Juan and Meyer, Richard L. 2007, "Introducing Rural Finance into an Urban Microfinance Institution: The Example of Banco Procredit, E L Salvador.

Bugada, Kathy. 2007, "Using Palm Pilots to Reduce Microfinance Transactions Costs: An example from Safe Save in Bangladesh".

Consultative Group to Assist the Poor (CGAP), "CGAP-advancing financial access for the world's poor".

Dauner Gardiol, Isabelle. 2004, "Mobilizing Savings-Key Issues and Good Practices in Savings Promotion".

Dellien, Hans and Lynch, Elizabeth, 2008, "Rural Finance for Small Farmer: An Integrated Approach".

Food and Agriculture Organisation of the United Nations (FAO), 2005, "Microfinance and forest-based small-scale enterprises".

International Fund for Agricultural Development (IFAD), 2004, "IFAD Rural Finance Policy".

Milligan, Walter, 1994, "11 Reasons for the possible failure of a Revolving Fund". Paper presented at Japan Program/INDES 2001 Conference "Priorities and Strategies in Rural Poverty Reduction: Experiences from Latin America and Asia," Japan.

Pearce, Douglas and Reinsch, Mika, 2005, "Small Farmers in Mozambique Access Credit and Markets".

Pearce, Douglas, 2003, "Buyer and Supplier Credit to Farmers: Do Donors have a Role to Play? Portail Microfinance.

Quiros, Rodolfo. 2007, "Agricultural Value Chain Finance: Summary of the conference, Costa Rica, May 2006.

Ramm, Hans, 2007, "Policy for Financial of Sector development: Update 2007", Rural Finance Learning Centre.

Swiss Agency for Development and Cooperation (SDC), 2007, "An Era of Innovation: Thirty Years of SDC's Involvement with Rural Finance in India.

Wenner, Mark D. 2002, "Lessons Learnt in Rural Finance, The

Experience of the Inter-American Development Bank".

World Bank, 2001, "Agricultural Technology and Land Management Project, IDA Credit No. 2536-NI", World Bank Report No. 2254.

World Council of Credit Union, 2003, "A Technical Guide to Rural Finance: Exploring Products".

Zeller, Manfred. 2003, "Models of Rural Finance Institutions. Invited lead paper for the International Conference of Best Practices in Rural Finance, June 2-4, 2003.

2

India's Foreign Trade in Agricultural Products under WTO Regime

Sakeer E. and Rais Ahmad

It is impossible for any country to be completely self-sufficient. If every country could be self-sufficient and produce all the things it needed (whether goods or services) with the same cost effectiveness and efficiency as another country, then there would be no need for trade and international markets. Since there are considerable differences between countries, it is more advantageous and beneficial for countries to enter into an exchange, with each one specializing in the production of those goods or services, in which it has a comparative advantage and this holds good in agriculture too (Samuel). The agricultural sector has been playing an important role in international trade and in the changed market scenario under the WTO; and in the milieu of the AoA, international trade in agriculture has assumed a larger significance (Samuel).

Despite being an agrarian economy, where the agricultural sector provides employment to approximately 60 percent of the population and contributes 25 percent to the GDP of the country, India has remained a marginal player in world agricultural trade. Currently, it has a share of less than 1 percent of the world trade in agriculture. The share of agricultural products including coffee, tea and fisheries in the total exports of India was around 10.5 percent in the year 2010-11.

The World Trade Organization (WTO) is the only global international organization dealing with the rules of trade between nations. The establishment of the World Trade

Organization (WTO) in 1994 has brought tremendous changes in the agricultural trade in India. It is also important for India's development policy, to raise agriculture growth to contribute to increasing the country's share in world trade. While the liberalization reforms during this period clearly mark a significant departure from the protectionist past, India has a long way to go in integrating its vast agricultural sector into world markets (Premachendra, 2005). In particular, recent efforts to reduce barriers to trade in agricultural and food products, including tariffs, quantitative restrictions and other trade barriers, through the Uruguay Round, provide opportunities for enhanced export performance for both traditional and non-traditional products.

World Trade Organization (WTO) has developed certain provisions related to agricultural sector to help in regulate trade between nations. With the advent of WTO and its provisions in agriculture bring many opportunities and put many serious challenges as well.

However, India has a long way to go in integrating its vast agricultural sector into world markets. The present papers is structured as follows: the following section provides the general background on India's position in world agricultural trade and the next section describes the reform process over the past decade, paying attention to issues in the implementation process and the unfinished reform agenda.

Agriculture, identified as one of the potential sectors for harnessing India's competitive advantage in international trade, is geared towards achieving the country's overall trade target of 1 percent or more share of world trade. While making the country self sufficient in the last few decades, agriculture has also played a significant role in earning foreign exchange through export of traditional items like tobacco, tea, coffee, cashew spices, raw cotton, basmati rice, etc Indian agriculture is highly export competitive and that trade would help the country to harness its vast export potential (Gulati et al. 1994).

Exports of Agricultural Products

Agricultural plays an important role in our international trade too. The main agricultural commodities which are exported are tea, oilcakes, fruits and vegetables, spices, tobacco, animal hair, and vegetable oils. There is a huge scope of international trade, because it is now exporting rice and wheat to many countries including China. There is a vast scope of exporting the cereals to various countries by raising exports of agricultural goods with the opening up of the domestic market rapidly. India will make its presence felt on the world trade scene. However, reforms in agriculture sector have been rather slow during the first phase of economic reforms. The government has been cautious since the debates on the impact of trade reforms on food security, small farm economy, environment, and so on, are inconclusive.

Nearly one-seventh of the country's total export earnings accrue from the agricultural sector. Although Indian agriculture has grown at a reasonable pace, the majority of farmers are holding less than 2 hectares of land, net cropped area is stagnant assured irrigation system is highly inadequate and for a large number of farmers, the gains from application of the science and technology is yet to be realized. Therefore, it would be a challenging task to maintain the growth in agricultural production.

In terms of exports, India is not a major player in the world agricultural commodity market except in the case of a few commodities such as rice, spices, soya meal, cashew, tea and coffee. As there is persistently increasing trade deficit for the country as a whole, increasing net exports of agriculture is a significant contribution to the country's economy. Hence, in the coming years, India has to focus on its agriculture not only to meet the domestic demand but also to increase its export to help the rest of the economy (NAAS, 2001).

India's agri-exports can be divided in to three broad categories as given below:

1. Export of raw products.

2. Export of semi raw products.
3. Export of processed and ready to eat products.

The export earnings from traditional export commodities like tea, coffee, spice and tobacco suffered mainly due to a sharp fall in international prices, as the quantum of exports in most cases did not drop. Global liberalization of agriculture following WTO was further seen as a great opportunity for promoting exports (Rajiv R. Thakur, 2005).

Major Export Markets of India

The impact of the WTO on India's agriculture has been studied by Dr. Ramesh Chand, of National Centre for Agricultural Economics and Policy Research (NCAP). He has found that the first three years, after the implementation of the WTO agreement, witnessed a major spurt in agriculture exports. The study attributes the slow-down on agro-exports and sharp rise in imports to the decline in global prices of almost all major agriculture commodities after 1997. This crash was due partly to the cyclical nature of international prices and partly due to increased global competition in agro-export because of liberalising trade. The situation was aggravated by an increase in the already high farm subsidies in the developed countries.

The Indian non-Basmati rice and wheat could not face global competition. The export of oil meal, the second biggest export item after marine products, also suffered a setback due to a decline in global prices.

Though there is some recovery in the price cycle in the recent years, yet the current level of prices of above mentioned commodities is 15 to 44 percent lower than the prices prevailing in the beginning of WTO. Because of this decline in prices in post WTO period, developing countries' exports were badly hit and several countries like India were taken aback by import influx of commodities, in which they thought they had strong competitive edge. This caused adverse impact on farmers' income, employment and livelihood security. The decline in international prices happened contrary to the projections that implementation of WTO AoA would result in reduction in subsidies and thus, increase in cost of production and prices.

Indeed, one of the most important arguments put forward in support of trade liberalisation was that it would improve the prospects of an export-led growth process in agriculture (Ramakumar). But the study says another result as the share of agricultural exports in total merchandise exports declined from 21 percent in 1996-97 to 12 percent in 2003-04.

There were considerable variations in export performance of various commodities. Non basmati rice and wheat could not face global competition. Export of oil meal, which was the second biggest item of export after marine products, suffered serious setback due to decline in international prices and quantity of exports. Export earnings from traditional group consisting of tea, coffee, spices and tobacco, suffered mainly due to sharp fall in international prices as quantity of export in most cases did not decline. Export (value in US$) of marine products, and groups of livestock and horticultural products maintained the tempo of growth, continuing from pre-WTO period . This shows that post WTO situation was favourable to export of high value food products. Export of cotton almost dried up in the post WTO period due to increased demand from domestic textile industry and decline in domestic production. Sugar exports remained occasional as the surplus arose temporarily. This scenario of India's agricultural exports indicate that future negotiations should focus on taking advantage in export of high value food products.

At present, India is a net food exporter. In fact, its share of exports in world exports is greater for agriculture than it is for manufactured products, the total export share being less than one percent.

Global agri-trade in the post-WTO regime is full of challenges for developing nations like India. While the new regime promises opportunities out of the expected reduction in subsidies and decrease in quantitative restrictions (QRs), developing nations face threats from developed markets in form of non-trade barriers like Sanitary and Phyto sanitary Measures (SPS) and Technical Barriers to Trade (TBT). Addressing these challenges with the intention of harnessing the competitive advantage of its agriculture sector, India has initiated strategic plans which involve farmers, the private sector, and governmental and non-governmental agencies. All put together, these plans have shaped up in the form of Agri-export Processing Zones (AEZs) (Rajiv, 2005).

It was expected that under WTO, the entry of agricultural products from India in the world market would be without much restrictions owing to market predictability, reduction in aggregate measures of support (AMS) and export subsidies. Undoubtedly, there are significant improvements in India's agriculture exports after the WTO.

India's agri-exports face certain constraints that arise from conflicting domestic policies relating to production, storage, distribution, food security; pricing concerns etc. unwillingness to decide makes Indian supply sources unreliable. Higher domestic prices in comparison to international prices of products of bulk exports commercially less comparative. Market intelligence and creating awareness in international market about quality of products need to be strengthened to boost agricultural exports.

Case Study: Export of Rice, Wheat, Cotton and Sugar

For India rice, wheat, cotton and sugar are the important agricultural commodities. India is the largest producer of these commodities in the world. Rice and wheat are the major staple food in the country.

A minimum support price (MSP) for rice and wheat is announced every year by the Commission for Agricultural Costs and Prices taking into account the cost of production and aiming at protecting the agricultural producers from any sharp fall in farm prices. India follows the procurement and stocking policy for public distribution of rice and wheat and the Central Government plays an important role in setting up the national agriculture policy in spite of the fact that agriculture is a state subject in the Constitution, therefore the state governments have to give their concurrence to the prices and policies drawn up by the Central Government. Cotton production policy in India has been oriented towards promoting and supporting the textile industry.

Thus, prior to the recent reforms, the producers were heavily taxed by export controls aimed at providing low cost cotton to domestic textile mills. To encourage producers, the Government of India (GoI) announces a minimum support price for each variety of seed cotton. India is also the largest consumer of sugar in the world. GoI had totally decontrolled the sugar industry in 2002-03 subject to futures trading becoming fully operational. A MSP is also annually announced for sugarcane. Gulati and Kelly (1999) estimated that India would be exporting tons of rice, wheat and cotton with globalization of agriculture. Gulati (2002) also found that India would be competitive in exporting sugar and cotton if trade liberalization takes place. Indian agriculture is getting connected to the world agriculture but the price fluctuations due to trade distortions are keeping the country away from being competitive (Mittal).

Subsidies in developed countries have affected the trading pattern of a number of Indian agricultural products. The example of rice can be pertinent here. During the early 1990s, India removed restrictions on rice exports. Following the removal of export restrictions, India emerged as a major rice exporting country. However, just after the Asian crisis, international price of rice started declining.

International prices of cereals towards the year 2000 and 2001 turned out to be almost half of what they were in the beginning of WTO. This happened when India was having very large stock of rice and wheat. Tariffs turned out inadequate to keep a check on import of cereals and India had to resort to QRs on imports of food grains to keep a check on cheap imports. Important lessons from this experience are that India was not able to safeguard domestic production against imports with usual tariff when international prices went low. In order to deal with this kind of situations, India needs either high bound tariff, so that applied tariffs can be raised appropriately, or, special safeguards to regulate imports of sensitive products.

Challenges in Exports of Agricultural Goods

After the introduction of economic reforms in 1990-91, the share of agriculture exports increased (with fluctuations) to 20.50 percent in 1996-97. Thereafter, it has continuously fallen down with share at 10.5 percent in 2010-11. One of the reasons (among many others) has been the failure of poor quality Indian agri-products to clear the international standards of quality and control set by the CAC, by EU, Japan and US. Therefore, it is necessary that SPS clauses are properly understood and better quality and control are introduced in the agri-export of the country, otherwise the exports of this category will continue to fall even in the future.

Based on this logic net trade is an indicator of self reliance. Trend in agriculture trade shows that post WTO trade liberalisation did not help much in export growth but it resulted in sharp and continuous increase in import (Ramesh, 2005).

In practice India do not have enough capacities to produce and to fulfil the developed countries markets due to many reasons. Among the many reasons is that the India has lack of efficient technology and skills. These factors result in a high cost of production in the domestic market as well as in the world markets. Furthermore, India is producing similar products among themselves and even similar with the products produced by the developed countries where technologies are better developed and efficient. Consequently Indian output prices become more expensive than those of the developed countries. Besides that, the qualities of the outputs are also better for the developed countries compared with India. As a final result, demands for the domestic products in the India become lower relative to the demand for the developed countries' commodities.

Contingency trade policy and non-tariff measures (NTMs) continued to act as significant barriers to exports from developing countries, but with somewhat reduced intensity. Such barriers are considerably stiffer for products with lower value addition and lower technological content (e.g. agriculture, textile's and leather products), which are of major interest to developing countries like India. With its diversified manufacturing and export base, India has been one of the major users as well as one of the major targets of anti-dumping measures in the world. During January-June 2006, 20 WTO members reported initiating a total of 87 new investigations, down from the 105 initiations in the corresponding period of 2005. India reported highest anti-dumping initiations with 20 new initiations (taking each country as one case) followed by European Communities (17) and Australia (9). As far as imposition of new final anti-dumping measures during the first half of 2006 is concerned, China reported applying the largest number (15) followed by Turkey (11), India (8) and Egypt (7).

India's Imports under WTO Regime

While increase in exports is of vital importance, we have also to facilitate those imports which are required to stimulate our economy.

The impact of W.T.O on agriculture was severely felt by India as cheap imports have frequently hit the Indian market, causing shock waves among the agriculture producers. Between 1998-999 and 2000-01, the average annual import of farm products rose by about 64 percent. Vegetable oils account for the largest share of imports followed by vegetables, edible fruits and nuts, and inputs for the textile industry: cotton, wool, and silk (Munisamy, 2008).

In the case of imports, liberalisation of trade in the initial years of implementation of WTO agreement did not cause much difficulty because international prices of bulk products were quite high in the first three post WTO years. Subsequently, as international prices started falling, India's imports started rising. Level of imports doubled in three years between 1996-97 and 1999-00 (Ramesh, 2005). In contrast to exports, agriculture imports witnessed 80 percent increase in US$ value after 1996-97. The post-WTO period showed increase in ratio of imports to GDP whereas ratio of exports to GDP for agriculture sector followed small decline. This shows that post WTO period has been adverse to export but favourable for imports (Neelamegam et al., 2008).

India imports valued at US$ 7.5 billion in FY 2007/08. Imports are growing and include vegetable oils, wheat, pulses, raw cashews, dry fruits, cotton, wool, hides and skins, and fruits and vegetables. India is the largest global importer of pulses (beans, peas, and lentils) and soybean oil and second largest importer of palm oil. In 2006-07, India emerged as the third largest importer of wheat in the world, with total imports of around 6.2 million tons. Imports declined to around two million tons in 2007-08. However, no U.S. wheat was imported due to the Indian government's unreasonable phyto-sanitary requirements.

Total U.S. agricultural exports to India in 2007 were valued at US$ 483 million, up 30 percent from 2006, driven mostly by almonds, apples, peas, cotton, and planting seeds. With pulse imports from the U.S. valued at a record US$ 60 million in 2007, India was the largest market for U.S. pulses. Imports of various consumer-oriented food products from the United States, including fruits like apples and grapes are increasing, reaching a record US$ 265 million in 2007.

Composition of imports shows that most of the increase in agriculture imports took place due to increase in import of edible oil. Vegetable oils accounted for more than three fourth of total increment in agriculture imports in the post-WTO period. The other items whose imports increased significantly are pulses, spices, cotton, and wood and wood products (Ramesh, 2005).

In case of imports, liberalisation of trade in the initial years after the WTO did not result in any perceptible spurt because global prices were high. But subsequently, when global prices began to fall, India's imports started rising. The level of imports nearly doubled in the three years between 1996-97 and 1999-2000. This downturn in global prices continued even in subsequent years. The composition of items in the import basket indicates that edible oils accounted for the bulk of the increase in total agro-imports. The other items clocking significant increase in imports include pulses, spices, cotton, wood and wood products. The study has also revealed that the spurt in the imports of vegetable oils, and wood and its products has depressed their domestic prices, adversely impacting indigenous production.

By 2002, almost all quantitative restrictions on agricultural imports had been abolished. Tariffs are now the principal means by which India protects its domestic industries and agriculture (Prema-Chandra Athukorala, 2005).

Challenges of Indian Trade in Agricultural Products

1. Inefficient technology, lack of infrastructure, institutional bottlenecks, policy intervention by the government and other factors are also responsible that India's surplus are not export competitive and deficit are not import competitive.
2. Water scarcity is growing, and is fostering conflicts. In many countries, developed water sources are almost fully utilized, even as agricultural demand for water is expected to increase drastically in the future. Thus, cooperation dominates but there have been numerous conflicts as well, mostly at the local level. Countries can resolve water shortages by importing food, and thus implicitly importing water. But with increased trade protectionism, this

efficient solution is undermined, and local water conflicts may increase (Joachim, 2009).

The food price inflation in India has been traditionally much higher than those in developed countries such as the United States, Japan or Canada making it harder to export agricultural processed products. The general inflation in India during 1998-2003 had been about 4.5 percent and a similar trend continued during the later periods of 2004-2006. Clearly, if imports were going to reduce the food prices further, it would not be increasing the welfare of farmers, unless substantial gains are made through food based manufacturing export-enhancing strategies.

The primary cause of the recent food-price inflation was the severe drought of 2009, which caused a downturn in food production in the third quarter of 2009-10 and the expectation of the resultant price rise itself fed further into the inflation. Government reacted carefully by easing up imports of relevant food grains and sugar and also releasing wheat and rice from the stocks held by the Food Corporation onto the market. High fuel prices in the international market also contributed to the higher food prices by increasing transportation costs.

Mitigating the risks facing the low-income, resource-poor and subsistence farmers associated with price declines, price volatility and predatory competition and other market imperfections, including the huge amounts of production and trade-distorting subsidies provided by some developed countries to their agriculture sector, remains paramount. Therefore, along with other developing countries, particularly its alliance partners in the G-20 and G-33, India has been emphasizing that the Doha agricultural outcome must include at its core:

1. Removal of distorting subsidies and protection by developed countries to level the playing field.
2. Appropriate provisions designed to safeguard food and/or livelihood security, and to meet the rural development needs of developing countries.

Subsidies in developed countries have affected the trading pattern of a number of Indian agricultural products. The example of rice can be pertinent here. During the early 1990s, India removed restrictions on rice exports. Following the removal of export restrictions, India emerged as a major rice exporting country. However, just after the Asian crisis, international price of rice started declining

When international prices are low there is deluge of imports into India, and, when international prices are high there is no symmetric spurt in exports due to quality problems. Therefore, quality competitiveness has never been so important as in the current liberalised trade environment. It is imperative that farmers and entrepreneurs engaged in post-harvest handling and food processing will have to commit themselves wholeheartedly to food quality management (Deodhar, 2001). The world is witnessing a sharp decline in food commodity prices. The FAO Food Price Index (FFPI) dropped by almost 13 percent (or 24 points) in October 2008, falling to its lowest level since August 2007. The sharp decline in the index reflected the rapid decrease in international prices of all major food commodities. This is quite worrying for Indian farmers because their cost of production keeps rising with the increasing corporatisation of agriculture while they are not getting good return for their produce.

Despite being blessed with the largest cultivable landmasses on Earth, India's agricultural productivity is one of the lowest in the world. 70 percent farmers have no access to credit, extension services and technology. Half of India is susceptible to soil erosion and 80 percent of India is drought prone (Rahul).

The Productivity Paradox

The most striking paradox in Indian agriculture is the paradox of productivity. Although productivity gains were sustained in the 1990s after the liberalization process began, the yield rates for most of the crops in India are far below comparable rates in a number of other countries.

Except for tea, coffee and citrus, India's yields are lower than the world average. We have huge areas under rice cultivation, but the average yields in several countries are much more than ours. Egypt has over three times India's yield rates in rice. In all major crops, India's productivity performance seems to lag behind other nations.

It is this productivity paradox that is perhaps the most severe limiting factor in India's competitive position vis-à-vis agricultural trade.

1. Adoption of modern agricultural practices and use of technology is inadequate, hampered by ignorance of such practices, high costs and impracticality in the case of small land holdings.
2. Illiteracy, general socio-economic backwardness, slow progress in implementing land reforms and inadequate or inefficient finance and marketing services for farm produce.
3. The average size of land holdings is very small (less than 20,000 m^2) and is subject to fragmentation, due to land ceiling acts and in some cases, family disputes. Such small holdings are often over-manned, resulting in disguised unemployment and low productivity of labour.
4. Since 1995, public investment in agriculture has experienced a secular decline, while input subsidies (on fertilizers, power, and canal irrigation) have been rising. In the early years of economic reforms, an attempt was made to arrest and reverse these trends, but this effort could not be sustained. As a result, the gap between investments and subsidies kept widening. Today, input subsidies together with food subsidies, amount to roughly five to six times the public investment in agriculture. With a burgeoning subsidy bill and shrinking public investment, the growth impetus for agriculture has been declining. Private investment in agriculture has been increasing, yet it has not fully compensated for the loss from falling public

investment (Joachim et al., 2005).

5. However, the food price inflation in India has been traditionally much higher than those in developed countries such as the United States, Japan or Canada making it harder to export agricultural processed products. After remaining at an average annual rate of 9 percent during 1981-90 and almost 11 percent during 1991-98, the food price inflation has come down to the level of these countries only recently. The general inflation in India during 1998-2003 has been about 4.5 percent and a similar trend continued during the later periods of 2004-2006. Clearly, if imports were going to reduce the food prices further, it would not be increasing the welfare of farmers, unless substantial gains are made through food based manufacturing export-enhancing strategies.
6. The facts about horticulture and dairy products reveals the dominant position of India in fresh fruit and dairy production, and the huge export potential that remains to be tapped.
7. Perhaps the most significant impact that trade liberalisation had on Indian agriculture was the sharp fall in domestic prices of many commodities after the mid-1990s. In the background of greater integration between domestic and international markets, domestic prices of cotton, tea, coffee, spices and many fruits and vegetables fell following a sharp fall in the corresponding international prices. Due to the absence of quota controls as in the pre-WTO period and the ineffectiveness of low tariffs, the surge in the imports of various crops contributed in different degrees to the decline in their domestic prices (Bhalla, 2004; Ghosh, 2005).

Problems Created by Developed Countries

However, with agriculture subsidies and export promotions, developed countries have dominated the world agriculture market historically. More than 67 percent of world food exports during 2001-03 originated from the high-income countries, while countries such as India where more than 65 percent people survive on agriculture, contributed only 1.1 percent of food exports (Kaliappa et al., 2006).

Table 2.1: Farm Support in OECD Countries before and after WTO

S.N	Value of Output	1986-1988	1995-1997	2002-2004
1	Total Value of Production OECD	597.00	769.00	740.00
2	Producer Support Estimation OECD	243.00	252.00	254.00
3	Market Price Support: OECD	188.00	170.00	156.00
4	Percentage Producer Support Estimation	37.43	29.62	30.35
5	Producer Support Estimation in EU	1o1.70	117.60	114.27
6	Producer Support Estimation in USA	36.40	26.30	40.41

Source: Agricultural Policies in OECD Countries, OECD 2005.

Industrialized countries systematically use subsidies to skew the benefits of agricultural trade in their favour. Various studies have consistently reported that agricultural surpluses in rich countries, generated through protection and subsidies and then dumped onto world markets, have hurt agricultural development in developing countries. The actions of some of the developed countries were a serious cause of concern for India where agriculture is the largest private sector enterprise with over 110 million farmers and workers, contributing about 25 percent of the country's Gross Domestic Product. It is argued that WTO is now imposing rules which are costly to implement and inappropriate for existing infrastructure in developing countries like India.

Sanitary and Phyto-sanitary Measures (SPS) and Technical Barriers to Trade (TBT) of Agricultural Goods.

While the new regime promises opportunities out of the expected reduction in subsidies and decrease in quantitative restrictions (QRs), developing nations face threats from developed markets in form of non-trade barriers like Sanitary and Phytosanitary Measures (SPS) and Technical Barriers to Trade (TBT).

SPS problems have been attributed to many causes, which can broadly be identified as the lack of quality regulatory and supervisory systems, as well as the lack of necessary guidelines for agricultural and food production. Regulations inconsistent with international standards are a basic flaw, which need to be addressed first. This results in producers often misusing chemical fertilizers, pesticides and antibiotics (Rajiv, 2005).

How to Make Indian Agriculture Globally Competitive under the WTO Regime

1. **Improving Farm Productivity:** One of the major reasons for the poor yields per unit of land area is the inefficiency in the use of fertilizers and poor cultivation practices leading to imbalanced nutrition. The use of modern farming practices on a wider scale and integrated nutrient management practices are essential if India's farmers wish to produce crops in line with the observed global standards of quantity and quality. A consequent increase in Productive efficiency, upon following the best practices in crop nutrition, would enhance value-added activities in agriculture through agro-processing and exports of agricultural and agro-based products. These activities in turn would increase income and employment in the industrial processing sector. Thus, globalizing agriculture has the potential to transform subsistence agriculture to commercialized agriculture and to improve the living conditions of the rural community. When addressing the

need for balanced fertilization using specialty farming techniques, it must be borne in mind that the potential for increasing productivity of land already under cultivation is far greater than that for bringing more land under cultivation. The inherent limitation in this approach is that plant nutrient deficiencies in both irrigated and rain-fed farms will increase. The problem of eliminating these deficiencies is already a major problem today and it will aggravate in the future. Integrated nutrient management has spin-off benefits as well. The most crucial is the improvement in the plant physiology that builds levels of resistance and reduces the incidence of disease and pest attacks. Increasing resistance through efficient nutrition programmes can thus reduce the application of harmful (and expensive) pesticides and make farming more productive, sustainable and environmental friendly. Sanitary and phytosanitary standards prescribed by developed nations prescribe very low permissible levels of pesticide and chemical residues. Thus, developing resistance makes the farm produce more 'saleable' in world markets.

With a view to making Indian agricultural products more competitive in the global markets, the Union Cabinet decided to remove the cess on exports. Former Union Commerce and Industry Minister Kamal Nath told that the decision to remove the cess on exports of agricultural produce would make our exports more competitive and profitable. He said a cess would only make the exports more expensive and uncompetitive. Agricultural exports already formed a significant proportion of India's total exports and there still remained a vast untapped potential for exports from this sector.

2. **Growing Use of Genetically Modified Seeds:** It is commonly said that if the last decade was one of Information Technology (IT), then the next decade will be one of Bio-technology (BT). India is known as a potential

future bio-tech hub for the world. Seeds constitute, on average, 60 percent of the Input costs for farmers. Use of genetically modified (GM) high yielding varieties of seeds has the potential to usher in the 'Next Green Revolution'. The farmers in the USA have adopted GM seeds on a large scale leading to an estimated benefit of US$ 6 billion. Our neighbour, China, similar to us in most respects, has achieved remarkable productivity increases of 30 to 40 percent from the use of GM seeds. However, lack of political will, myopic views of scientists on the "perceived" ill effects instead of on demonstrated bio safety risks and cumbersome procedures have worked to ensure that India has effectively missed the Genetic Revolution. Fortunately, the pendulum has finally swung in favour of adopting GM seeds starting with non edible cash crops (like Bt cotton) and then hopefully, Indian farmers will be allowed move with caution towards food crops. Uncertainties exist now more with regard to the speed and extent of adoption of new-generation seeds. Agri-biotechnology has proved useful to farmers to increase yields, controlling pests, insects, weeds, creates drought resistance, flood resistance and allows cultivation in "stressed" soils. Genetically modified seeds promise high yields.

A major challenge confronting Indian agriculture is the development of transport infrastructure and processing systems to efficiently integrate agricultural production on millions of small farms with consumers and traders in cities and ports. Hoda and Gulati point out that for southern Indian states it is at times cheaper to import wheat by ship from Australia than overland from Punjab, illustrating the significance of a country's size, location, and infrastructure with respect to agricultural production, trade, and consumption.

3. **Reducing Dependence on Monsoons:** India's agriculture is still completely at the mercy of the Rain Gods.

Changing seasons are now more of a certainty. It is imperative that Indian agriculturists brace themselves to meet this 'certain' uncertainty. Overcoming this rain dependence is crucial to assure markets that India can continually supply farm output at cost effective prices. Recent campaigns by International organizations and government policy initiatives, including subsidies and extension services, have led to the slow but steady rise in practices like drip irrigation, hydroponics and greenhouse cultivation. This reduces phenomenally the need for water in agriculture and promotes conservation of this scarce resource. It also makes farming more productive with the delivery of the right quantity of nutrients at the right time, in the least available cost, using the optimum volume of water. Moreover, rainwater harvesting projects are penetrating the hinterland. Recently, India has seen a few remarkable examples of successful micro-irrigation projects. Kuppam in Andhra Pradesh was developed as one such show-case by the A.P. Government and leading manufacturers of such systems from Israel. Despite having rocky topography, scanty rain over the past four years and poor soil, Kuppam has farms successfully producing almost every conceivable crop using drip irrigation systems. Agro-forestry initiatives, wasteland cultivation using hardy crops needing least quantity of water, are also underway to reduce the dependence on the monsoons, while at the same time, sustaining revenue from agricultural land.

4. **Interlinking India's Rivers:** The idea of linking India's rivers which had been lying dormant for a long time, has acquired prominence recently with the Supreme Court having decreed that the rivers of India shall be linked within ten years. A task force has been set up to work out the modalities of this largest, most ambitious infrastructure project on Earth. The Court has also mandated the allocation of the ₹ 5,60,000 crore required for this project.

However, the uncertainty in the entire issue stems from the vociferous debate raging in "green" lobbies that have christened this project as "technological arrogance of the worst kind" while making an attempt to alter India's geography. Other constraints include finding a source for collecting the mandated funds, environmental impact assessment, cost benefit analyses and investment feasibility.

It is uncertain whether India's rivers will be linked in as grandiose fashion as decreed by the Courts or thought of by planners. However, it is certain that limited links will be created in a definite time frame. For instance, work on the Krishna-Godavari river link within Andhra Pradesh has already begun. The benefits are obvious: water management, flood control, reduced dependence on the monsoons, growth of irrigation, drought resistance, increase in area under cultivation and employment generation. Irrigation is undoubtedly the key to India's economic future. The linking of rivers will assure availability of water for agriculture, guarantee crop cycles, reduce uncertainties in agriculture, unify the country and ensure prosperity for generations to come.

Export of raw products like cotton, wheat, sugar, coffee and tea is likely to become very competitive and India would be required to re-look into the benefit of promoting export of these commodities.

5. **Change in Eating Habits of Indians and in the Developed World:** India is growing in affluence. This affluence is not just restricted to cities having a middle class with ever growing purchasing power, but also covers rural areas. The Indian Market Research Bureau (IMRB) estimates that 49 percent of Rural India figures in the middle/upper income segments. Increased affluence has led to an increased demand for more nutritive foods, including fruits and vegetables, in addition to staple cereals and pulses. Vegetarianism is also growing in

popularity, as is the recent trend the world over. This is a trend increasing observed in the developed nations. This change in eating habits has made it feasible for farmers to diversify into horticultural crops. Horticultural crops have relatively high nutrient requirements. Moreover, they are also labour intensive to cultivate and generate rural employment.

6. **Growing Access to Information:** Awareness amongst India's farming community is increasing, as a direct corollary to increasing literacy and open access to global information. 3 percent (1066 lakh households) are estimated to have at least 2 graduates. 16 percent have at least one member who is SSC/HSC+. This is equivalent to 5 times the population of Singapore, 3 times Israel and a little less than all of Australia. A wealth of scientific knowledge about soil chemistry and physics exists, as well as extensive geo-data on the distribution of soil types. Thanks to modern technology, telecommunication and satellite television, this information is being brought directly to the farming communities and through rural tele-centres, electronic information resources and other media including video presentations. The "digital divide" remains a very real constraint, but the rapid spread of mobile phones and satellite technologies opens new vistas for extending access to relevant knowledge. In fact, the communications revolution has comprehensively networked rural India. Apart from leapfrogging directly into the era of mobile telephony, 70 percent of farmers have access to televisions and an even higher 86.8 percent listen to the radio. This has "opened up" the farmer's world and has ensured growing access to relevant information.

7. **Revamping the Domestic Distribution of Food Stocks and Dismantling the Subsidy Regime:** Domestic restrictions on the inter-state movement of farm products have created a situation where food grain stocks are piled

up in warehouses of the government while parts of the country are starving. These food grain stocks are piled up to satisfy the fiscal orthodoxy of antiquated planning mechanisms which do not hold much ground in today's open, integrated markets. The original reform agenda had in fact envisaged increased public investment, to be financed by input subsidy cuts which were also expected to improve input-use efficiency and discourage environmentally unsustainable practices. Since this effectively meant taxing farmers in regions with better infrastructure, resistance was sought to be muted by increasing support prices to remove `negative subsidies' in trade. In the event, subsidies have not reduced but support prices have become too high to be consistent with free international trade at present low world prices. With this option no longer available, the talk is again of freeing markets. But import controls have gone, very few restrictive orders are actually being invoked under the Essential Commodities Act, and removal of remaining export restrictions is unlikely to yield much in global market conditions. This leaves only thornier and earlier unthinkable options, such as dismantling the support price/PDS system and allowing the corporate sector to take over trade, processing and extension. It is this possibility, and implications for income distribution, that disturbs critics the most. However, it remains true that in a small farm economy such as India's, economies of scale require larger entities to provide critical inputs in technology, infrastructure, marketing and risk management. There are only three ways this can be done: by Governments, through cooperation among farmers, or by allowing corporate control. Much of the problems of the past decade stem from the fact that even as farmers have been exposed to new uncertainties from liberalization, the state has retreated from these responsibilities and left cooperatives sidelined without creating conditions for corporate entry.

Rather than the current drift, many would prefer greater corporate involvement.

8. **Development of New Generation Irrigation Systems:** There is a tremendous opportunity in the indigenous development of economical irrigation systems suited to local conditions. Most of the irrigation systems are currently imported from countries like Israel, Australia, Japan, etc. Few international companies specializing in the design and development of irrigation systems have set up subsidiaries in India. However, a major hindrance is the high cost of installing these systems coupled with a phase out of government subsidy schemes supporting such installations. Even in areas where micro-irrigation systems were installed on full government subsidy or using 'soft loans' from rural banks, inadequate and ineffective training to farmers have caused the systems to remain largely unused. This is a huge national waste and a well structured, co-ordinated effort to develop easy-to-use, low cost systems coupled with systematic training to agriculturists and farm labour would ensure the wide adoption of this technology.
9. **Development of New Generation Seeds:** This is an area where several Indian companies have taken the lead. Research and Development focused on the introduction of hybrids suited to Indian conditions is underway in various parts of the country. However, the opportunity of increasing harvests using genetically modified, hybrid seeds can be completely exploited only with a mass awareness campaign to negate the anti-propaganda that has plagued the growth of this concept.
10. **Diversification and Change in Cropping Pattern:** Progressively reduced support prices for cereal crops have made farmers to consider the cultivation of new generation crops. The change is widely observed in agriculturally progressive states like Andhra Pradesh and Maharashtra where land is being used to cultivate horticultural crops

(fruits and vegetables), oilseeds and pulses. Some state governments like in Andhra Pradesh, have even resorted to quasi-coercive tactics like denying the release of canal water to farms cultivating traditional cereal crops like paddy. Once the resistance to the change is overcome, cultivators realize a much higher realization from their land since these new crops are much more remunerative and even have export potential. Some cultivators have gone a step further and diversified into the cultivation of exotic crops including medicinal herbs and spices like turmeric and vanilla where the potential for revenue generation is enormous. Crop diversification is a strategy that emanates from the realization that it is makes ample economic sense for India to import cereals from other countries in South East Asia (like Thailand) where the cost of production is much lower and use its land and labour resources to produce crops like edible oil, fruits and vegetables that are more expensive to import. This exploits the competitive advantage of nations to improve agriculture's balance of trade and makes farming in India more profitable.

11. **Specialized, Environment-friendly and Cost-effective Integrated Nutrient Management Solutions:** Increasing farm productivity per unit of land area using the global best practices will necessitate intensive agriculture. Harvests can be sustained in the long term with intensive use of land only if crop nutrition is balanced. Add to this, the specialized and enhanced nutrient needs of genetically modified seeds. These seeds promise high yields. However, to ensure bumper harvests, these crops need higher levels of nutrition. For crop productivity to be sustained, nutrition requirements are relatively much higher for GM seeds than traditional seed varieties. Nutrition solutions recommended are almost always specialties due to their demonstrated effectiveness the world over. Growing awareness towards using GM seeds

will directly affect the demand for specialty balanced fertilizers. Moreover, global markets expect an elimination of harmful chemical residues in farm output. This requires a reduction in the rampant over-use of pesticides. For this, the plant will need to be made healthy with balanced nutrients. This is the only way, other than biological control of pests, to decrease pesticide use through increasing resistance.

12. **Contract Farming and Co-operative Agriculture:** Land holdings in India are extremely fragmented. This fragmentation increases with every successive generation that inherits the land. Fragmentation also makes the land uneconomic in size and scope. It severely limits the adoption of mechanization and new age farming practices. Moreover, farmers with limited output have very little bargaining power while negotiating prices for their yield. Recognizing these problems, there is a move towards co-operative agriculture. Farmers in close proximity have started forming co-operatives, pooling their land and resources to jointly produce crops. This allows pooling of resources and gives rise to economies of scale. Moreover, it permits better utilization of land and joint efforts to improve productivity. In certain areas, companies have stepped in to organize farmers to adopt contract farming as a model to improve the economics of farming. Companies enter into forward contracts with the farmers, undertaking to lift the entire output of a specified quality and quantity at a price which is set well in advance. This effectively assures the farmers of a set price for their yields and effectively hedges them against price fluctuations. In turn, the companies are assured of their inputs of raw materials at fixed prices. In several cases, the companies provide all the inputs (seeds, fertilizers, pesticides, credit, technology, etc.) to the farmers to ensure the quality of the harvests in line with their specifications. This has gone a long way in reducing some of the risks associated with agriculture and

effectively improving productivity.

13. **Planned Allocation of Land for Cultivation of Crops and Specialization:** A common tendency of Indian farmers is to blindly produce that crop which has been most remunerative in the previous season, with little or no consideration for future demand patterns. If a certain crop has been comparatively more remunerative to a farmer in the area, most farmers who become aware of this windfall change their own cropping pattern due to the "herd mentality". This consequently leads to a glut in the market with over-supply of a particular crop in the following season, causing a crash in prices of that commodity.

    An opportunity exists to use effective demand forecasting techniques for various crops to allocate land most effectively to avoid peaks and valleys in farm output. This will keep farm gate prices relatively stable as supply will remain 'managed' in line with demand forecasts. Developed nations like the US, effectively use such a system of planned allocation of land to create pockets of excellence for producing certain crops in certain parts of the country. This creates regional specialization and increases efficiency in agriculture.

14. **Harnessing the Power of Technology to Improve the Economics of Farming:** The spread of technology into the hinterland can be very effectively used to disseminate real time information to agriculturists on ruling international and domestic prices for various crops, forward prices in commodity exchanges, world demand forecasts, weather information, crop management practices, etc. ITC's e-Choupal initiative is an experiment to harness the power of technology to link India's farmers using an Infotech network. Farm productivity can be enhanced by using the information available to make structured, meaningful and rational choices. There are unlimited opportunities for similar initiatives to harness the power of technology which will go a long way in

improving the economics of farming. In an inter-connected world, such information will certainly prove invaluable to the farmers.

15. **Food Processing:** Food processing is an opportunity for Indian agriculturists to move a step up in the value chain. It allows the farm sector to effectively overcome the 'commodity syndrome' and add value to their output by processing the output as per the requirements of the market prior to sale. This could entail packaging, branding, processing into higher value products (like potatoes into packaged chips, tomatoes into ketchup or ready-to-eat soup, etc.) that permit much better realizations. Food processing is also an industry that could provide employment opportunities.

    To encourage exports of agricultural products, the government has set up agricultural export processing zones.

    FAO suggested that developing countries and less developed countries should expand their range of agricultural exports. They continue to export a narrow range of primary commodities that are highly vulnerable to instability of demand and deteriorating terms of trade. Extension programs should address the issue of expanding the range of agricultural exports (FAO, 2001).

    Indian public investment should increase higher manner. India currently invests only about 0.5 percent of its agricultural GDP in agricultural research, compared with 0.7 percent in the developing countries as a whole and as much as 2-3 percent in the developed countries. These figures suggest that government has been systematically under investing in a sector that offers a high social return and that there is considerable scope for diverting incremental outlays to priority areas in research. In R&D, India had a successful record of importing high yielding seed varieties and adapting them to local conditions during the late 1960s and 1970s, an effort that led to the Green

Revolution. Although there is still ample scope for increasing rice and wheat yields, especially in the water-abundant eastern belt, the Green Revolution has been stagnating in the northwest states of Punjab, Haryana, and western Uttar Pradesh, as well as in the southern states of Andhra Pradesh and Tamil Nadu. To keep pushing the production frontier outward, India must invest in new technologies and the institutions to accompany these technologies.

The new agricultural technologies on the horizon are largely biotechnologies. Indian policymakers, scientists, and regulators have long supported the development of biotechnology (including genetic modification) that provides new crops favourable to India's climatic areas and is suitable for use by farmers in rural communities. One of the most important technologies in the Indian context is one that produces drought resistance. Developing biotechnology appropriately, however, will require effective research and reforms of the regulatory structure and process, duly recognizing the local and international debate on biotechnology, particularly regarding genetically modified (GM) crops. In this context, setting up a body like the National Biotechnology Regulatory Authority (NBRA) would enhance regulation of biotechnology in India. Investments in advanced crop technologies for Indian farmers will pay off only if there are accompanying investments in infrastructure. The connection of India's villages to information and communications technology is an important component of these initiatives. The private sector can be the key driving force, and many corporate giants have already entered rural areas with a view to expanding business. But public policy should facilitate these investments in rural areas by removing controls on private investment as well as by offering tax concessions for investing in rural areas, in order to improve poor communities' access to education, market information for farmers and other small businesses, and service information.

Conclusion

Despite impressive gains and some milestone achievements in few select agricultural commodities, India still has a long way to go in making its agricultural exports making more competitive in the world market. Liberalisation and globalisation of world trade regimes in agriculture products has certainly opened many new opportunities for a country like India, with it's near self-sufficiency in agricultural inputs, relatively low costs of labour and its diverse agro-climatic profile, which can support production of wide range of agricultural export products. However, India needs to raise the level of productivity and quality standards to international levels, which is one of the major challenges, following dismantling of quantitative restrictions on imports and with adoption of WTO agreement on agriculture.

While a beginning has been made in partly freeing the global agricultural trade from the constraints of stifling tariff and non-tariff barriers, considerable effort still needs to be taken up to neutralize the developed economies from resisting agricultural imports from the developing world and bring down the level of protection and subsidies to bring greater parity in terms of trade. India's challenges on the global agricultural trade front are thus, both internal as also external in nature. While required changes in the external global trade environment will take longer time and greater collective effort of nations, India needs to initially focus on improving its internal situation in the agricultural sector, by rebuilding its competitive advantages so that it can present stronger positions when it comes to negotiating either with WTO or other developed countries.

FAO suggested that developing countries and less developed countries should expand their range of agricultural exports. They continue to export a narrow range of primary commodities that are highly vulnerable to instability of demand and deteriorating terms of trade. To increase the export of Indian agriculture farmers should know the maximum about the EXIM policy, programs and schemes, price policy, seed policy and statistics at the Indian agro portal and harvest benefits from India, world's second largest producer of food and a country with a billion people.

From canned, dairy, processed, frozen food to fisheries, meat, poultry, food grains, alcoholic beverages and soft drinks, the Indian agro industry has dainty areas to choose for business. In India there is good prospect of increasing the trade because of huge customer for buying the agricultural products. An average Indian spends out about 50 percent of his/her household expenditure on food items.

With a population of over 1 billion and a 350 million strong urban middle class and their changing food habits, India needs to pay equal attention to what it agrees to do in its own market and economy and what other countries commit to do in their markets.

Instability of international prices has negatively affected export performance of a few crops in which India is internationally competitive. NPC based analysis carried out Hoda and Gulati highlights that India has demonstrated competitiveness in three temperate zone crops—rice, wheat and cotton. However, exports of these crops have been sporadic because of low international prices faced by these commodities since the mid 1990s. I can also point out that India can emerge as a competitive supplier of sugar and dairy products if international market distortions caused by the policies of support and protection pursued by some of the developed countries can be eliminated.

There is a possibility that as a result of the sustained decline in commodity prices, producers of some agricultural crops in India may become uncompetitive even at the domestic level. Higher returns from some export oriented cash crops like tobacco and sunflower have lured even smaller farms to undertake cash crop cultivation at the expense of traditional crops including foodgrains. This is a risky move because these farmers are now totally dependent upon the revenue form the cash crops even for their domestic consumption. International prices for cash crops are volatile and they fluctuate wildly from year to year. Every now and then, low prices of these commodities lead to heavy losses for farmers. The farmers who do not maintain a cushion of self-produced food-grains to support them, such losses can create huge food security problems. In southern part of India, there have been numerous cases of farmer suicides because of this reason.

India is yet a developing country, India is still dependent upon the US and EU markets for exports and imports. No country can live in isolation and therefore international trade, exports and imports are part of the modern day economies. However generally, there has been a surplus in agricultural trade over the years. The trade surpluses in terms of value was ₹ 17805.82 crore in 2004-05, and ₹ 28777.38 crore in 2005-06 respectively.

To face the WTO challenge, productivity has to be increased. It is estimated that there is a potential to increase productivity per unit of land area by 25 percent by using irrigation, balanced nutrition programmes and agri-technology, including genetically modified seeds. Moreover, to face the challenge of cheap imports, revenue per unit of land needs to be enhanced immediately along with a reduction in cost of production. This is possible by using global best practices in integrated crop management. To face the export challenge, similar economics will come into play. However, there is a further restriction placed on presence of pesticide and other chemical residues.

India needs to identify the major markets to which it can export its agricultural produce at maximum returns in terms of foreign exchange. The major markets for the Indian agricultural products are the developing counties and not the developed countries. We need to improve our exports to the existing large markets and also identify emerging markets. There is a need to constantly monitor the identified markets, which are existing or are emerging, to recognize their changing demands and accordingly modifying our domestic policies, taking into account the changes in the world markets, so as to gain through exports.

Export controls were maintained on agricultural raw materials such as cotton, timber, hides and skins, and leather in order to keep their domestic prices low and thus protect domestic industry.

As a net exporting country, India stands to gain from increase in international prices, which is possible only if we relentlessly fight for reduction of domestic subsidies and support and export subsidies in the developed countries. (Neelamegam).The global agriculture trade regime under the World Trade Organization (WTO), that came into force 10 years ago in 1995, has led to an increase in the import of farm products into India rather than boosting exports.

We need to make an effort to improve India's price competitiveness, which would definitely help India capture a higher share in the world imports. There are various reasons why India lags behind in being price competitive. One of the factors, which contribute to the higher pricing of products, is that the farmer does not sell his products directly into the main market. Various intermediate steps are involved, before the produce finally comes to the ports for export, due to which, the price becomes higher and ultimately in the international markets, Indian agricultural products are more expensive, thereby losing their competitiveness.

There are restrictions on direct sales from farm to traders, sales outside regulated markets and disposal of forestry produce raised on farmlands. These need to be appropriately changed to reduce transaction costs, reduce the share of the middlemen and to give a wider choice to farmers in production and sale. We need to capture major markets of the world like the markets of EU, Japan and US, identify the top imports of these countries and evaluate our major exports to these countries.

It is expected that reduction in export subsidy and domestic support to the agricultural sector by the developed countries may lead to a decrease in production in those countries and, therefore, will give scope for expansion of exports from the developing countries. India, with its cheap labour, diverse agro-climatic conditions and large agricultural sector can definitely gain through expansion of international trade in agricultural products. However, the concerns relating to quality of products for seeking markets in the advanced countries needs to be addressed on an urgent basis.

India has to develop, diversify and add value to its agricultural production structure and become competitive, and thus compete in international markets including in exporting high value products. Some issues in this regard included the rising cost of inputs which impinged on competitiveness of agricultural production and exports; non-tariff barriers such as SPS; and constraints in financing and other instruments including measures identified, for example, by the Monterrey Conference on Financing for Development and the World Summit on Sustainable Development.

This paper argues that India should engage more actively in the multilateral trading system. Because engagement can facilitate domestic reform and enhance access for India's exports. India is now at a critical juncture. It is an increasingly willing reformer, but confronted by opposition to reform domestically. At the same time, market access in areas of major export interest remains impeded. Multilateral engagement pits these two elements against each other constructively. On the one hand, domestic reform would be facilitated if the government could demonstrate that there were payoffs in terms of increased access abroad. The gainers from the increased access, be they exporters of textiles, software, professional services or other products, could represent a countervailing voice to groups that resist reform. On the other hand, the need to demonstrate external payoffs to secure greater openness at home makes India a credible bargainer, and could help induce trading partners to open their own markets.

India has a large potential to increase its agricultural exports in a liberalized world provided it can diversify a significant part of its agriculture into high-value crops and in agro processing. This would depend first on undertaking large infrastructure investment in agricultural and agro-processing as also in rural infrastructure and research and development. India has not only to create export surplus but also to become competitive through increased efficiency of production in agriculture. The potential for exports would also depend on freeing of agricultural markets by the developed countries (Malik).

India being a net exporter in agriculture products, it has more to gain from the trade reforms. It has sufficiently high bound rates on most of the products and therefore, flexibility can be ensured against unfair competition. India does not have to worry about its subsidy, as it is already below the required line and it also does not have any domestic support to recon with. All these place India in an advantageous position. Moreover, the ongoing negotiations are likely to yield enough flexibility in product choice and tariff selection Exports of agricultural commodities, particularly foodgrains, accelerated in this period. For example, for the fist time since independence, India has been a net exporter of foodgrains consecutively for the last six years, net exports amounting, on an aver-age, to around 1.8 million tonnes per annum (Government of India 2001).

In the light of this evidence, the fears being expressed in certain quarters that import of foodgrains under the new liberalised trade regime is having a dampening effect on the foodgrain prices in the country is totally misplaced. It is true that, recently, the post-harvest prices of wheat and rice have been ruling below the mini-mum support prices in certain markets. The present glut in the foodgrains market cannot be adequately explained by the import of wheat to the extent of 2.8 million tonnes during 1997-98 and 1998-99 when government had imposed a ban on wheat exports and opened up imports at zero import duty. A plausible explanation is that there has been a steep rise in procurement prices in the recent period, when there has in fact been a downward trend in international prices.

The minimum support (procurement) prices of wheat, for example, were raised by 45 percent within a period of three years ending 1999-2000 [Commission for Agricultural Costs and Prices 2000]. Procurement of foodgrains reached an all time high of 19.7 percent of net production in the year 2000 [Government of India 2001]. Moreover, whereas the per capita availability of foodgrains was rising at the rate of 1.2 percent per annum during the 1980s, it has declined at the rate of 0.28 percent per annum during the 1990s [Government of India 2000]. This suggests that the trend of a decline in per capita consumption of foodgrains and the diversification of the consumption basket in the richer states and among the upper consumption groups, already in evidence in the 1970s and the 1980s according to the National Sample Survey data [Rao 2000], seems to have been reinforced in the post-reform period of 1990s owing to the availability of a wide variety of non-agricultural goods and services as well as the rise in the relative prices of food grains.

Whereas the consumption of food grains among the bottom 30 percent of population was still rising in the 1980s, though slowly, the steep rise in food grain prices in the 1990s may have dampened consumption among these poorer sections. It almost appears that the country is caught in the 'advanced country syndrome' of support prices feeding on themselves leading to reduced consumption, embarrassing surpluses, reduced incentives for diversification of agriculture and for the adoption of cost-reducing technologies.

This evidence does not lend credence to the view that trade

liberalisation would endanger India's food security. Achievement of effective food security when enough stocks of foodgrains can be accumulated, thanks to India's comparative advantage in respect of major cereals, hinges basically on raising the purchasing power of the poor through the generation of employment opportunities. If the prices of foodgrains at the moment are out of the reach of the poor, it is not due to the rise in exports but to the steep rise in procurement and issue prices.

References

Athukorala, Prema-Chandra. (1998). Trade Policy Issues in Asian Development. London: Routledge.

Bhagwati, Jagdish. (1993). India in Transition: Freeing the Economy. Oxford: Clarendon Press.

Bhalla, G.S (2004).Globalisation and Indian Agriculture, State of the Indian Farmer: A Millennium Study .Volume 19 of thee 27 Volumes sponsored by the Ministry of Agriculture, Academic Publishers ,GOI.

Braun, Joachim von. (2009). Threats to Security Related to Food, Agriculture, and Natural Resources–What to Do?. In conference strategic discussion circle EADS, Berlin March 26.

Chand, Ramesh and Seema Bathla (2005), Concerns, Viewpoints and Consensus WTO Agriculture Negotiations and South Asian Countries, South Asia Economic Journal.

Chand, Ramesh (2005). India's Agriculture Trade during post-WTO Decade: Lessons for Negotiations. In: seminar 'Off the Blocks to Hong Kong: Concerns and Negotiating Options on Agriculture and NAMA' CENTAD, 22nd July, 2005, New Delhi.

Chandrasekhar, C.P, Jayati Ghosh and Parthapratim Pal (2003). The Green Barrier to Free Trade. Date retrieved 12 march 2010 . available at: http://www.networkideas.org/focus/feb2003/fo03_Free_Trade.htm.

Gulati and Sharma, (1994), Agriculture under GATT: What it holds for India. Economic and Political Weekly, Vol. 29, pp. 1857-1863.

Gulati, A. and T. Kelley (1999): Trade Liberalization and Indian Agriculture. New Delhi: Oxford University Press.

Kalirjan, Kaliappa and Kanhaiya Singh (2006).India and the WTO's Agreement on Agriculture (AoA). In: International Association of Agricultural Economists Conference, Gold Coast, Australia, August 12-18, 2006.

Kaur, Kuljit and Arneet Kaur. (2009). WTO Trade Regime and Indian Agriculture: Challenges, Implications and Recommendations. In Ahmad, Rais (ed.). WTO and Indian Agriculture: Opportunities, Problems and Challenges, New Delhi: Mittal Publication.

Malik, R.P.S, "Indian Agriculture: Recent Performance and Prospects in the Wake of Globalization" Date retrieved February 2009. Available at: http://nrlp.iwmi.org/PDocs/DReports/Phase_01/04.percent20WTOpercent20andpercent20agriculturepercent20-percent20RPSpercent20Malik.pdf.

Mirchandani, Rahul (ed.). Building Competitiveness in an Inter Connected World: Opportunities and Challenges in Agriculture.

Mittal, Surabhi "Will OECD Agricultural Trade Reforms Impact India's Crop Prices and Farmers Welfare? Date retrieved: June 2010. Available at: http://www.ecomod.org/files/papers/854.pdf.

Neelamegam R. and Dr. Thilaha Mary Antony, (2008), Enhancing efficiency of Indian farming in the face of globalization. Date retrieved May 2010. Available at: http://www.aima-ind.org/ejournal/articlesPDF/DrRNeelamegamA452120082679709.pdf) NSS Survey (1999-2000).

Prema-Chandra Athukorala. (2005). Agricultural Trade Policy Reforms in India. South Asia Economic Journal, 6; 23.

Ramakumar R. Indian Agriculture under Economic Reforms: A Preliminary Review. Date retrieved March 2009. Available at: http://www.networkideas.org/ideasact/jan09/PDF/Ramakumar.pdf.

Ronald, Bindu Samuel (2006). Market Access for Agricultural Products. Date retrieved January 2008. Available at: http://www.scribd.com/doc/136506/Market-Access.

Srinivasan, T.N. (1998a), India's Export Performance: A Comparative Analysis'. in Isher J. Ahluwalia and I.M.D. Little (eds), India's Economic Reforms and Development: Essays for Manmohan Singh, pp. 197-228. New Delhi: Oxford University Press.

Thakur Rajiv R., 2005, "The Changing Global Agri-trade Regime and Indian Agri-exports" Global Business Review http://gbr.sagepub.com.

Upton, M, (2000). The Livestock Revolution Implications for Smallholder Agriculture: a Case Study of Milk and Poultry in Kenya. Report for AGL Service. Rome: FAO.

3

Micro Credit to Rural Poor: Role of NGOs

Salini K.

Introduction

Poverty eradication is one of the key issues emphasized in all the economic and academic discussions globally. It has been estimated that more than one-sixth of the global population live in extreme poverty who struggle even for mere survival. Around 70 percent or more of the Indian population live in rural areas. At about 33 percent of the GDP (Gross Domestic Product) is contributed by agriculture and related activities of rural people. [1] The rural people are easily exposed to untimely death, frequent ill health, accident and injuries, malnutrition, underweight and related health issues. The people who earn an income of US$ 1 per day is considered to be BPL (below the poverty line), according to UN standards. [2] Then India would have 35 percent population to be considered to be under BPL.

191 nations of UN have signed the UNMDGs (United Nations Millennium Development Goals) in the year 2000. The first goal of the same is to alleviate extreme poverty and hunger all around the world. This indicates the fact that poverty is the greatest challenge that the global society face. UNMDGs has set out a target to its member nations including India, that to reduce the total population by half living with an income a dollar a day by 2015 , so as to eliminate extreme poverty by 2025. [3] Many developmental policies have been changed and renovated to achieve the same by the Government of India, both at the Central level and at the State levels. As a response to the first goal of MDGs (Millennium Development

Goals), India targets to reduce the percentage of poverty from 37.5 percent (year 1990) to 18.75 percent by 2015. In order to gain this absolute figure, the role of NGOs is considered to be important by the authorities. They undoubtedly have the institutional capacity to reduce poverty through group lending mechanism. Compared to the Governmental agencies, NGOs have operational and comparative advantages.

Micro Finance: An Effective Tool for Poverty Reduction

Microfinance is the provision of small loans and financial services at the affordable cost to vulnerable poor, especially in rural areas. There are two elements on the subject of rural credit. These are: (i) an emphasis on savings and other financial services apart from loans; and (ii) professional management of small loans and savings programmes. These loans are intended to encourage production and consumption of the rural poor by the establishment of micro enterprises. [4]

Access to formal credit and freedom to use the same are considered to be the major constraints faced by the poor especially in rural areas. Though they access credit from informal money lenders, the interest rates charged by them is exorbitantly high. In India, initiatives like Self Employed Women's Association (SEWA) recognized the same even before. Though the topic was well considered and discussed by many experts throughout the world for several years, a special emphasis was given at the first International Women's Conference in Mexico, in 1975. This was further strengthened by the Micro Credit Summit Campaign in 1997, which had 'reaching and empowering women' as the second important goal after 'poverty reduction'.

In recent debates and discussions, microfinance has been promulgated as an effective measure to attack poverty. Therefore, it received a lot of consideration from both policy makers and academic experts. During the past ten years, microfinance programmes have been extensively initiated by developing countries all through the world. [5] The celebrated examples are Grameen Bank of Bangladesh, Banco Sol in Bolivia and Bank Rakyat in Indonesia. Among these, the Grameen Bank, established in 1976 based on 'Group Lending' system has been widely adopted in developing nations. Group Lending is a lending mechanism, in which a group of people contributes to a collective fund and the same is distributed to the members of the group on a need basis. The group as a whole is responsible for the repayment of the loan with interest issued without any collateral. This is known as 'Group Liability and peer pressure' lending system.

Microfinance in particular has grown through four distinct developmental periods (Table 3.1) [6]:

Table 3.1: Developmental Periods of Microfinance

Period	Features
Early 1980s	Many MFIs has better repayment policy
Early 1990s	Only few MFIs began covering all the costs
Mid 1990s	Good MFIs began to get significant contributions from commercial channels.
Today	MFIs try to satisfy both objectives

Source: Compiled by the author.

A study conducted by the World Bank in collaboration with the Bangladesh Institute of Development Studies, showed that the Grameen Bank not only reduced poverty and improved the welfare of participating households, but also enhanced the household's capacity to sustain heir gains over time. [7] In a typical year 5 percent of Grameen borrowers—representing 125,000 families—rise above the poverty level. [8] Many times, the term microfinance is limited to the narrow definition of 'micro credit for micro enterprises'. But apart from micro credit, it includes a wide range of services like savings products, insurance, remittances and some services in similar nature.

Role of SHGs in Poverty Eradication in Kerala

In Kerala, the state of poverty is comparatively less with

other states in India. As per the official declaration by the Planning Commission, the poverty level has come down to 9.4 percent (year2000) from 25.73 percent (year 1994). [9] This can be considered as substantial decrease in poverty level of the State. The major role played by SHGs (Self-help Groups) and NGOs (Non-Governmental Organizations) cannot be ignored while analyzing the reasons for the substantial decrease of poverty. Such groups have put significant efforts in bringing them up economically, socially and culturally.

The mission like 'Kudumbashree' has helped the rural poor a lot for their economic progress. [10] It really proved to be a successful method for eradicating poverty through generation of employment and income. There are similar other measures with the same objective initiated by different authorities like NABARD, women cells, different state level committees etc. NGOs effectively manage "community groups" and encourage group lending. Benefits of the group will be divided and distributed to the individual members of the group. The role of NGOs is not confined only to an advisory or supervisory level, but they can also assist the poor by involving in their personal and legal issues, health problems, education, vocational job oriented training to increase their entrepreneurial skills. Among other several developmental agencies, NGOs try to decrease poverty by simultaneously enhancing the financial and economic profile of the rural people with special focus to women and underprivileged. [11]

Likewise, the role that is performed by banking sector in India to distribute micro credit to the needy deserves considerable appreciation. Increasing access to credit to the poor has always been a major consideration of Indian Planning. Hence, the idea of Financial Inclusion came forth. Financial inclusion is defined as the process of ensuring access to timely and adequate credit and financial services by vulnerable groups at an affordable cost. [12] Financial Inclusion and availability of credit have traditionally eluded the poor. No development can take place without a strong and sound banking system. We are using the banking system to broaden and deepen democracy by requiring that a certain proportion of loans shall be extended to borrowers in priority sectors such as farmers, students and self help groups. [13]

However, surprisingly, the reach of commercial banks in rural areas is still not adequate. Despite the wide network and specific poverty alleviation programmes, which aim to create self employment opportunities through bank credit, a very large number of poor and deprived remain out of formal bank finance. But financial inclusion helped to shift the focus of commercial banking from 'Class banking' to 'Mass banking'. [14] This has even strengthened with the introduction of SHG-Bank Linkage programme of NABARD in 1992. Under the 1992 guidelines, the SHG functions as a joint liability group, replacing other collateral for the loans. The collateral free loans increase progressively to up to four times the level of the group's savings deposits. SHG thus linked became 'micro-banks' able to access funds from the formal banking system. Launched in 992 in India, early results achieved by SHGs promoted by NGOs such as MYRADA, led NABARD to offer refinance to banks for collateral-free loans to groups. The programme envisages three broad models of linkage (Table 3.2).

Though the outreach of SHG-Bank linkage programme seems to be impressive, the flow of funds for poverty alleviation from the banking sector accounts for only less than 5 percent of the banking system's disbursements for agriculture and allied activities. [15] Thus, while the SHG programme has made notable progress in providing loans to largely poor families, it has not made a significant addition to the credit flow to the rural areas.

Review of Recent Literature

The failure of commercial banking to provide financial services to the poor coupled with disadvantages of using informal markets are major rationales for intervention in the market for financial services at the micro level (Asyraf Wajdi Dusuki, 2008).

Consequently, microfinance emerged as an economic development approach intended to address the financial needs of the deprived groups in the society. The term microfinance refers to "the provision of financial services to low-income clients, including self-employed, low-income entrepreneurs in both urban and rural areas" (Ledgerwood, 1999).

Table 3.2: Types of SHG-Bank Linkage Models

Model	Name of the Model	Description
Model I	Bank-SHG-Members	Bank itself promotes and nurtures the SHG until they reach maturity.
Model II	Bank-Facilitating Agency-SHG-Members	Groups are formed and supported by NGOs or government agencies.
Model III	Bank-NGO-MFI-SHG-Members	NGO acts as both facilitators and Microfinance intermediaries. NGOs federate SHGs into apex organizations to facilitate inter group lending and larger access to funds.

Source: Information compiled by the author.

The emergence of this new paradigm was encouraged by the successful story of microfinance innovations serving the poor throughout 1970s and 1980s. The most quoted examples are Grameen Bank Bangladesh, the unit desa system of Bank Rakyat Indonesia, ACCION International in United States and Latin America and PRODEM, BancoSol's predecessor in Bolivia. The microfinance adopts market-oriented and enterprise development approach. It emphasizes institutional and programme innovations to reduce costs and risks and has greater potential to expand the financial frontier to the poor in sustainable manner (Littlefield, 2003).

Puhazhendi (1995) and Srinivasan and Satish (2000) studied the micro credit programme of the nationalized commercial banks in India and concluded that the intermediation of non governmental organizations (NGOs) and self-help groups (SHGs) in the credit delivery system reduced the transaction costs of both banks and borrowers.

The essence of conventional profit-maximization banks as financial intermediaries providing financial services to people hinge upon these two elements. As formal lenders, risk-averse banks would only be willing to lend if these two elements serving as a basis of trust exist in their reciprocal relationship with clients (as borrowers). For instance, the bank is able to assess the reputation of borrowers based on bank's intimate knowledge embedded in the clients personal accounts as well as other documented history of past borrower behaviour.

At the same time, the clients have material value such as properties or any valuable assets serving as collateral to pledge against risk. However, these two elements poised important impediments to the poor especially in the rural areas to access into credit market (Asyraf Wajdi Dusuki, 2008). The poor are usually perceived by the "profit-orientated" banks as high-risk borrowers due to inherent difficulties in assessing their creditworthiness at the same time their inability to provide collateral to pledge against any potential risk.

These traditional formal lenders faced with borrowers whom they do not personally know, who do not keep written accounts or "business plans" and who want to borrow small and uneconomic sums (Jacklen, 1988); thus exposing them to very high risks due to the inherent screening problems faced by the lenders at the same time make the project appraisal become too expensive (Rhyne and Otero, 1992). Most formal intermediaries like commercial banks also regard low-income households as "too poor" to save, thus further accentuates the risk of supplying credits to them (Adams and Vogel, 1986; Sinclair, 1998).

Furthermore, no insurer is willing to insure against possibility of non-repayment due to natural and commonest hazards afflicting small producers in developing countries; for example, drought, livestock disease and breakdown of equipment (Hulme and Mosley, 1996). The risk exposure in supplying credits to the poor clients is further exacerbated due to the inherent difficulty for the commercial financial institution to diversify their portfolio. For example, most of the rural clients who derive their incomes from agriculture need to borrow in the pre-harvest season, making it difficult for banks to diversify their portfolio (Zeller and Sharma, 1998).

The financing of micro enterprises has long been an intractable problem. Historically, their financing needs were met by the local groups, voluntary organizations, and moneylenders. In practice, these institutions provide a limited coverage due to shortage of resources. The concessionary credits by the state do not reach micro enterprises because they are pre-empted by the rich. Similarly, the formal banking institutions avoid lending them (Akhtar, 1997).

The word, micro credit, which was hardly heard before the 1970s, has now become a buzzword among money market operators. They include such diverse types of people: traditional moneylenders, pawnshops, friends and relatives etc., informal groups, conventional banks providing specialized credit, such as, agricultural credit, livestock credit etc., cooperative micro credit, and bank NGO partnership based micro credit and Grameen type micro credit or Grameen credit (Elahi and Danopoulos, 2004).

Cost Ford and South Malabar Gramin Banks

Cost Ford: Cost Ford has started its operations in the year 1985 has made tremendous contributions in the area of microfinance. The founder of Cost Ford is the former Chief Minister of Kerala, Mr. C. Achutha Menon. The Chairman is Mr. Laurie Baker. The Director is Mr. T.R. Chandradath. Their main activity is cost-effective construction of buildings and transfer of technology among poor people.

Cost Ford has 18 centres all over Kerala. But women Empowerment Activity is widespread mostly in Thrissur District. They have a tie-up with Kerala Agricultural University, Mannuthi, Thrissur District and NABARD mainly for their Training and Development activities. For their women Empowerment programmes, with the assistance of NABARD, they have disbursed more than ₹ 3 crore till now of which 70 percent is distributed for Productive Purposes and 30 percent is for consumption Purposes. [16]

Cost Ford is given a target of "one ward-one group", and they have achieved 3,000 SHGs within one year. All SHGs will be assisted by Cost Ford, in registration, training and weekly/monthly meetings etc.

The Concept of 'Sthreesakthi'

To study the effectiveness of micro financing as a potential tool to expose the entrepreneurial talent among the rural poor, Cost Ford a prominent NGO in Thrissur District with its flagship scheme 'Sthreesakthi' is considered. For this, the flow of funds to SHGs and the utilization part of the same are analyzed in detail.

The Poverty Eradication Mission of the State-'Kudumbashree'—is a much appreciated mission throughout the country for its efficiency and effectiveness. This has encouraged several other NGOs to develop and implement similar programs in different districts and villages. 'Sthreesakthi' is one of such programs implemented in Thrissur District. The scheme is also using the base idea of 'community lending' and 'group formation' technique for increasing the saving habits of its members. [17] It has already proven its potency in bringing the women together from diversified local areas under one umbrella. It is structured as a participatory approach. Sthreesakthi is a concept originated and launched by NABARD in the year 1998. On an experimental basis, it started its operations in Thrissur District.

For implementation, NABARD entrusted the responsibility in Cost Ford, a prominent NGO in Kerala.

Working of 'Sthreesakthi'

The idea was already there informally in the structure of groups in Churches etc. 'Sthreeshakthi' is a program under which a group is formed consisting of 10-20 unemployed women in one particular locality. These groups are in the form of Self-help Groups (SHGs). Opening a bank account is made mandatory for the registration of the group. That is considered as first and foremost stage towards Financial Inclusion. Initially, they are provided with funds by Gram Panchayat. Later, once they become a group, banks will be willing to grant loans for two reasons:

1. Ability to repay of the group is higher than individuals in the group.
2. The banks can satisfy their priority lending targets.

South Malabar Gramin Bank was the first bank which took initiative in granting such loans to SHGs at priority lending rate.

South Malabar Gramin Bank (SMGB)

The bank has started its operations in the year 1976 with its head quarters at Malappuram, Kerala. It comes under the purview of Regional Rural Bank Act, 1976. It is one of the largest Regional Rural Banks in India in terms of total business. It has its operations in eight districts, with 228 branches and 9 area offices. It is sponsored and managed by Canara Bank by subscribing 35 percent of its share capital. The rest of the sharc capital is sponsored respectively by Government of India (50 percent) and Government of Kerala (15 percent). It enjoys a client base of nearly 2 million depositors and 1 million borrower clients. The Bank is rated as one of the 50 largest Micro Credit Institutions in the world. South Malabar Gramin Bank (SMGB) has also entered into the bancassurance business by becoming the corporate agent of Canara HSBC OBC Life Insurance Company Ltd. [18] A novel project "SNEHAGRAMAM" clubbing twin objective of Total Financial Inclusion and Money-lender-free villages is also launched. [19] In Thrissur, SMGB operates through 24 branches in the length and breadth of the district. Cost Ford has made arrangements with SMGB, East Fort Branch, Thrissur for assisting the financial needs of their clients.

Mode of Delivery of Micro Credit: Cost Ford and SMGB

Eligibility Norms for Bank Loans for SHGs: In general, the following steps will make the SHG eligible for funds from banks. These steps are closely monitored and reviewed by Cost-Ford in all stages.

As the SHGs are going through each of these steps under the strict supervision by Cost Ford, members of SHGs feel confident and chance of bank loan turning to bad debt becomes very less or nil. [20]

After careful analysis and verification in each stage, the bank, through NGO, will grant loans to the eligible SHGs. Each bank will have separate methodology for calculating eligibility for loans. SHGs under Cost Ford are provided loans mostly by South Malabar Gramin Bank (SMGB). Hence, the method they are using for calculating eligibility requires attention. They use the formula as given below:

The analysis of effectiveness of micro credit delivery is done with the help of studying the impact of flagship scheme of Cost Ford for micro credit and women empowerment called 'Sthreesakthi'.

The success and effectiveness of 'Sthreesakthi' are analyzed and presented in the following table. The analysis considers ten various SHGs which are engaged in diverse activities under the scheming leadership of Cost Ford. The data is collected and compiled from official records and personal interview with the concerned officials at Cost Ford.

Suggestions for Improved Performance

'Sthreesakthi' is a mission which effectively grouped

women together from diversified rural areas and guided them in a methodical manner. All the efforts taken by SHGs and NGOs are to be appreciated. Still certain suggestions have also come up from a primary analysis. These suggestions or recommendations can also be considered for their improved performance:

1. Adequate training in modern technologies like computers, telephone and other telecommunications networks etc can also be imparted.
2. Basic knowledge and training in accounting and general management may help them to perform better.
3. Educate them with proper timings for harvesting, fertilization needed, drip irrigation, deep ploughing etc for getting better output and higher profits.
4. Techniques of marketing (innovative ways to door-to-door selling) can be introduced to them.
5. Impart knowledge about proper pricing of the product as it is highly important for catching the market and withstanding with the existing competition.
6. Train the members to share mutually their resources like wells, machinery, raw materials which are common to them etc.
7. Teach them 4Ps of marketing in detail to add value to their work and to achieve more results.

Suggestions are only indicative. The authorities can do detail research for its operational issues. Applying the above as an experiment with say, any one group may give more clarity in its implementation.

Conclusions

The study throws light into the fact that efficient management and effective implementation can always produce good results. Poverty eradication missions like 'Kudumbasree', 'Sthreesakthi' etc. are proven to be very successful in bringing the poor families together and guiding them to generate income through productive entrepreneurial activities. The NGOs play a very integral role in combining and organizing the rural women into homogeneous group to engage themselves into heterogeneous, constructive revenue producing activities. The initiatives and efforts taken by all these non-profit organizations have to be appreciated. A big hand to them!

End Notes

1. "The Unchanging Face of Rural Poverty in India", a key note speech delivered by Dr. Abraham George at the GOPIO(Global Organization of People of Indian Origin) Conference in New York, 12th September, 2002. URL : http://www.tgfworld.org/critical-ruralpoverty.htm.
2. "A thin Indian line"–a write up by Dilip D'Souza, Digital Edition of Newsletter, India Together, dated 17 March, 2006. URL : http://www.indiatogether.org/2006/mar/ddz-povline.htm.
3. "The Roles of NGOs in Rural Poverty Reduction: A case of India and Indonesia, by Suharko, October, 2007, the working paper presented at International Symposium on Poverty Reduction policies held at Nagoya University, Japan. URL: http://www.gsid.nagoya-u.ac.jp/bpub/research/public/paper/article/160.pdf.
4. Hughes, David W., and Daniel Eades. "Micro credit." *Encyclopaedia of World Poverty*. 2006. SAGE Publications. 13 April 2010.
5. Hermes, Niels and Robert Lensink, "Impact of Microfinance: A Critical Survey", *Economic and Political Weekly,* Volume 42, Number 6, February 10, 2007, pp. 462-465.
6. Srnec K., "Conditions for the transformation of the MFIs from informal to formal types", *Agricultural Economics*, –czEch, *54*, 2008 (5), pp. 202-208.
7. Morduch Jonathan, "Analysis of the Effects of Microfinance on Poverty Reduction", *NYU Wagner Working Paper Series,* No. 1014, Issued June 28, 2002.
8. Yunus, Muhammad. November 1999. *The Grameen Bank.* Scientific American. 281(5). pp. 114-119.
9. "Case of Poverty amidst plenty states trends" –by Mr. T. Ramavarman URL : http://www.hindu.com/2007/10/08/stories/2007100859720500.

m.

10. "End of the Rainbow–The Saga of Kudumbashree- An article published by Mr. Jeemon Jacob in the publications–Kudumbashree. URL: http://www.kudumbashree.org/Publication/article_on_kudumbashree.htm.
11. Farhad Hossain and Tonya Knight," Financing the Poor: Can micro credit make a difference?, Empirical observations from Bangladesh", *BWPI Working Paper 38,* University of Manchester.
12. Rangappa K.B., Renuka Bai, Sandesh. A.L, SHG-Bank Linkage Programme And Financial Inclusion: Rural Household Study In Davangere District Of Karnataka, Working Paper, Indira Gandhi Institute of Development Research, www.igidr.ac.in/~money/mfc_10/K.B.Rangappa.pdf.
13. Chidambaram, Finance Minister of India, 2007, The Institute of Chartered Accountants of India, Source : http://www.icai.org/post.html?post_id=2418&c_id=240.
14. www.igidr.ac.in/~money/mfc_10/K.B.Rangappa.pdf.
15. Microfinance – Perspectives and Operations, Indian Institute of Banking and Finance: Macmillan India Limited, 2009.
16. Collected and compiled form the official records of Coast Ford.
17. Collected and compiled form the official records of Coast Ford.
18. "South Malabar Gramin Bank enters bancassurance biz", The Business Line, Friday, Jun 18, 2010.
19. The Official Website of SMGB. URL: http://www.smgbank.com/aboutus.htm , Referred on 25.06.10.
20. Collected and compiled from personal interview with the official-Cost Ford.

References

Adams, D.W. and Vogel, R.C. (1986), ''Rural financial markets in low-income countries: recent controversies and lessons'', *World Development*, Vol. 14, No. 4, pp. 477-487.

Asyraf Wajdi Dusuki, "Banking for the poor: the role of Islamic banking in microfinance initiatives", *Humanomics,* Vol. 24, No. 1, 2008, pp. 49-66, # Emerald Group Publishing Limited.

Hulme, D. and Mosley, P. (1996), *Finance against Poverty*, 1st ed., Vol. 1, Routledge, London.

Jacklen, H.R. (1988, 1989), ''Banking on the informal sector'', *paper presented at the International Conference on Micro enterprise Development*, Washington, D.C.

Khandakar Q. Elahi, Constantine P. Danopoulos (2004), Micro credit and the Third World: Perspectives from moral and political philosophy, *International Journal of Social Economics*, Vol. 31 No. 7, 2004, pp. 643-654.

Ledgerwood, J. (1999), *Microfinance Handbook: An Institutional and Financial Perspective (Sustainable Banking with the Poor)*, the World Bank, Washington, D.C.

Littlefield, E., Morduch, J. and Hashemi, S. (2003), *Is Microfinance an Effective Strategy to Reach the Millennium Development Goals?* , CGAP, Washington, D.C.

Muhammad Ramzan Akhtar (1997), "Partnership financing of micro enterprises", *International Journal of Social Economics*, Vol. 24 No. 12, 1997.

Puhazhendi, V. (1995), "Transaction costs of lending to the rural poor: non governmental organizations and self-help groups of the poor as intermediaries for banks in India", Banking with the Poor, Brisbane, available at: www.bwtp.org.

Rhyne, E. and Otero, M. (1992), ''Financial services for micro enterprises: principles and institutions'', *World Development*, Vol. 20, No. 11, pp. 1561-1571.

Sinclair, P.J.N. (1998), ''Why do the poor save so little?'', *Department of Economics Discussion Paper*, University of Birmingham, Birmingham.

Zeller, M. and Sharma, M. (1998), Rural Finance and Poverty Alleviation. Food Policy Report, *International Food Policy Research Institute,* Washington, D.C.

4

Financial Inclusion in India: Initiatives to Include the Excluded

Anamika Kaushiva

The Indian economy, with its vast socio-economic diversities and inequalities, requires policies for promoting necessary institutional transformation and affirmative actions in favour of the weaker and voiceless sections of the country, the toiling majority deprived from the opportunities of work and livelihood and struggling for survival. The growth trend of the Indian economy over the last few years has shown the beginning of a new phase of higher growth. From an average growth rate of around 6.0 percent for a quarter of a century, the growth rate has accelerated to 8.1 percent over the last few years. Along with declining population growth, growth rate in per capita income has also shown an upward trend. This growth process is will be sustainable only if the outreach of banking is spread out and the formal credit system adequately penetrates the informal financial markets.

The problems of backward agricultural sector, adverse terms of trade for primary commodities, chronic unemployment, and disguised employment and under employment continue to persist in the rural sector. Despite sixty years of planning and state intervention in economic affairs to correct the myopia and social insensitiveness of markets, structural, economic and social heterogeneity continues to exist.

Presently, the focus around the world is on sustainable development which calls for social sustainability, environmental sustainability and economic viability. This requires measures promotion of economic growth with positive social and environmental impacts i.e. inclusive growth. One important aspect of inclusive growth is financial inclusion. Enabling access to the structured and organized financial system to a major section of the population became an integral part of the Reserve Bank of India's agenda since 2004 with the adoption of financial inclusion policy. Measures of financial inclusion i.e. expansion of financial coverage for fostering faster economic growth in an inclusive fashion are being introduced for financial deepening at micro level.

This paper focuses on the definition and need of financial inclusion in the second section. The barriers to financial inclusion have been discussed in the third section of the paper. The fourth section focuses on the Indian banking scenario in reference to the deprived section of the economy and inquires into the nature and extent of the problem of financial exclusion. The fifth section deals with the major initiatives of the banking sector to address the problem of financial exclusion till the end of nineties. The major initiatives of RBI in the new millennium have been discussed in the sixth section.

The Background

The Indian economy, in the post-liberalisation period witnessed remarkable growth acceleration and the economy has been growing at an annual rate of 9 percent or so in the last 4 years. This growth acceleration has no doubt lead to a reduction in the percentage of the people below poverty line but it has also been accompanied with growing inter-regional, intra-regional and inter-personal inequalities in wealth and income. India still has the world's largest number of poor and world's largest number of undernourished children. The urban-rural difference is widening because the present economic growth process is not inclusive enough and is not sustainable for maintaining growth or stability or unity of the country.

The growth of the Indian economy on the "exclusive growth" pattern has led to development of two important features. One is a strongly segmented labour market consisting of a large segment of agricultural labourers, small-and marginal farmers, labourers confined to informal activities in household and small scale industries, living below or on the poverty line with hardly any access to protection or "risk management". Second feature is feeble participation or outright exclusion of a multitude that is of the illiterate or poorly educated, the unorganized, women, (subject to gender discrimination) from the political and social progress of the economy.

Inclusive growth encompasses ideas related to basic needs and equity. It focuses on broad-based growth which encompasses all strata of society. It seeks reduction in poverty and disparities of income and ensuring every one a basic minimum standard of living. Inclusive development requires economic inclusion, social inclusion, financial inclusion and political inclusion—exercise of all civic and political rights as well as accountability and transparency. All citizens must have an equal access to socio-economic services offered by government as well as by private organizations. The socio-economic policies financed out of the redistribution of income should benefit the unemployed, the illiterate and the underprivileged section both in the urban and rural areas. In this context access to finance by the poor and vulnerable groups is a pre requisite for poverty reduction and social cohesion. It has to become an integral part of the efforts to promote inclusive growth.

Access to affordable financial services, especially credit and insurance, enlarges livelihood opportunities and empowers the poor to take charge of their lives. Financial inclusion imparts formal identity, provides access to the payments system and to savings safety net. The financially excluded sections largely comprise marginal farmers, landless labourers, self-employed and unorganized sector enterprises, urban slum dwellers, migrants, ethnic minorities and socially excluded groups, senior citizens and women. Inclusive financial system, one that allows broader access to financial services, can lead to faster and more equitable growth.

The banking industry has shown tremendous growth in volume and complexity during the last few decades. Significant improvements in all the areas relating to financial viability, profitability and competitiveness have been witnessed. Between the years 2002-03 to 2005-06, the annual growth in retail credit was 46 percent: its share in overall bank credit increased from 6.4 percent in 1990-91 to 25.5 percent in 2005-06 indicating a move towards financial deepening. High industrial growth, a healthy corporate sector with high profit rates and high growth in terms of output also point towards financial deepening in the economy.

However, it is also true that the banks have not yet been able to include vast segment of the population, especially the underprivileged sections of the society, into the fold of basic banking services. Limited access to affordable financial services such as savings, loan, remittance and insurance services to the vast majority of the population in the rural areas and unorganised sector is a major constraint to the growth impetus in these sectors. Access to affordable financial services, especially credit and insurance, can enlarge livelihood opportunities and empower the poor to take charge of their lives. Such empowerment aid social and political stability, impart formal identity, provides access to the payments system and to savings safety net like deposit insurance and are critical for achieving inclusive growth; which itself is required for ensuring overall sustainable growth in the country.

According to the available data on the number of savings bank accounts and assuming that one person has only one account, (an assumption which may be incorrect as many persons could have more than one bank account) on an all India basis, 59 percent of adult population in the country have bank accounts–in other words 41 percent of the population is 'unbanked'. Currently, out of 19.9 crore households in India, only 6.82 crore households have access to banking services. In rural areas out of 13.83 crore rural households in India, only 4.16 crore rural households have access to basic banking services and in urban areas, only 49.52 percent of urban households have access to banking services. Over 41 percent of adult population in India does not have bank account. The 'unbanked' population is higher in the North Eastern and Eastern regions. Thus almost fifty percent of the population is financially excluded.

The high credit growth witnessed in the recent years is not matched with adequate deposit growth. Banks have been financing a large segment of credit expansion out of their own surplus investments in government securities. Whatever deposit growth has been registered, it is concentrated in the urban areas. This too implies existence of the problem of financial exclusion.

Financial Inclusion Defined

"Financial inclusion may be defined as the process of ensuring access to financial services and timely and adequate credit where needed by vulnerable groups such as weaker sections and low income groups at an affordable cost."

C. Rangarajan Committee Report, 2008

Financial inclusion means delivery of financial services at an affordable cost to the vast sections of disadvantaged and low-income groups. The various financial services include access to savings, loans, insurance, payments and remittance facilities by the formal financial system to those who tend to be excluded.

"Financial inclusion is delivery of banking services at an affordable cost to the vast sections of disadvantaged and low income groups. Unrestrained access to public goods and services is the *sine qua non* of an open and efficient society. As banking services are in the nature of public good, it is essential that availability of banking and payment services to the entire population without discrimination is the prime objective of the public policy".

Since finance performs the important functions of mobilizing savings, allocating capital and transforming risk by pooling and repackaging it, access to finance is can be defined as a public good which is as important and basic as access to safe water or primary education.

'Financial Inclusion' thus must also be categorized as a public good. A good is considered a 'public good' if it meets the conditions of non-rivalness in consumption and non-excludability. Financial inclusion meets the above two criteria to a large measure. There are a number of positive externalities of financial inclusion. One of the important effects is that one is able to reap the advantages of network externality of financial inclusion as the value of the entire national financial system increases. Further, fuller participation by all in the financial system makes monetary policy more effective and thus enhances the prospects of non-inflationary growth.

Barriers to Financial Inclusion

Extending banking and credit services in rural and informal urban areas is a daunting challenge, considering the grassroots level realities which are characterized by dilapidated soft and hard infrastructure like intermittent or no broadband and telecom connectivity, irregular power supply, unreliable public transport, sketchy road network, erratic cash flows among poor household and finally lack of a universally available and readily acceptable common identity proof. Serving low value retail customers in these geographies pose some operational, regulatory and viability challenges for banks. Banks are profit oriented entities and must be able to recover the costs which they incur in providing services like deposits, credit, remittance, insurance etc.

Otherwise the model would be unstable and may collapse one day. On regulatory part the Indian central bank does not make any incentivizing exceptions for banks based on branch size, location and business potential for operations like cash management, branch banking services, staffing, operating hours and the most important lending and interest rates on savings, which make banking with poor a costly and unremunerative affair for banks. There is a huge banking potential at base of the pyramid but it is required to overcome all of the identified barriers. Any successful model would essentially need to address all the barriers at the same time. This entails change in the approach of delivering services to the unbanked and under-banked areas.

The population to whom financial services are provided can broadly be divided into two groups- the users and the nonusers. The non users consist of those who do not use the services voluntarily due to cultural or religious reasons or because they do not see any need. They have access to financial resources but do not choose to use them. They do not constitute the problem of financial inclusion. On the other hand are those who are involuntarily excluded, who, despite their demand for financial services are deprived of them or do not have financial access. These constitute households with very low income levels and therefore high lending risks, people discriminated against on basis of social, religious or ethnic reasons, groups for whom the price and product features of services offered are unsuitable. There are many barriers to financial inclusion.

- **Physical Barriers:** These include barriers due to geographical location of a region. Regions in villages or interior rural areas are denied access to financial services due because of low number of bank branches. The average distance from banks is very high. Bank penetration into rural areas, hilly areas, border areas is very poor. Further banks do not use measures like e-finance, alternative delivery channels, and no branch bank outlets for loan applications to spread their outreach.
- **Documentation Barriers:** Access to bank finance often requires many documents like wage, slip, recommendation letters, proof of domicile i.e. formal proof for opening of account and sanction of loans. This becomes a barrier to

access to the illiterate and to those who do not have any fixed jobs and residence.

- **Barriers of Affordability:** The costs involved in opening and maintain an account, the annual fees, costly overdraft service fees often make the banking services unviable to the poor section and the population most in need of financial security and risk management is excluded.
- **Lack of Appropriate Products and Services for Low Income Groups:** Often the services offered by the banks do not match the local requirements and this leads to voluntary exclusion.
- **Illiteracy and Ignorance:** Members of the target groups are illiterate and ignorant about the policies and programmes of the Government.

Thus, these financial barriers deny the access to even the most basic financial products or give only restricted access to services like deposit and withdrawal of money with no flexibility of access and variety of services as are offered to the more affluent customers.

Besides these financial barriers, the financial exclusion of lower income groups is also because of demand and supply side constraints. From the supply side, operating cost is considered as one of the major obstacle in promoting financial inclusion. Salaries to staff, travelling expenses, commissions, staff welfare expenses, amortisation and depreciation, rent on hired buildings and other overheads—all constitutes the operating cost. These costs are critical for operating the formal banking system. From the demand side, the higher cost of financial services discourages inclusion. It is argued that the operating cost is higher for maintaining large number of account with lower average deposits. This results in the lopsided distribution of banks especially in favour of developed urban areas.

In the Annual Policy of the Reserve Bank for 2004-05, the Governor, Dr. Reddy observed-"There has been expansion, greater competition and diversification of ownership of banks leading to both enhanced efficiency and systemic resilience in the banking sector. However, there are legitimate concerns in regard to the banking practices that tend to exclude rather than attract vast sections of population, in particular pensioners, self-employed and those employed in unorganised sector. While commercial considerations are no doubt important, the banks have been bestowed with several privileges, especially of seeking public deposits on a highly leveraged basis, and consequently they should be obliged to provide banking services to all segments of the population, on equitable basis."

Voluntary and Involuntary Exclusion

Financial exclusion leads to increased travel requirements, higher incidence of crime, general decline in investment, difficulties in gaining access to credit or getting credit from informal sources at exorbitant rates, and increased unemployment, etc. The small scale enterprises suffer due to loss of access to middle class and higher-income consumers, higher cash handling costs, delays in remittances of money. Financial exclusion also leads to socio-economic exclusion due to the failure of the trickle down of the growth benefits to the rural sector the economy.

Extent of Financial Exclusion in India

Bank nationalization in India marked a paradigm shift in the focus of banking as it was intended to shift the focus from class banking to mass banking. Nationalisation of commercial banks in 1969 was followed by another measure to take the banking services to the poor–setting up of Regional Rural Banks. The branches of commercial banks and the RRBs increased from 8321 in the year 1969 to 68,282 branches as at the end of March 2005. The average population per branch office decreased from 64,000 to 16,000 during the same period. However, there are certain under-banked states such as Bihar, Orissa, Rajasthan, Uttar Pradesh, Chattisgarh, Jharkhand, West Bengal and a large number of North-Eastern states, where the average population per branch office continues to be quite high compared to the national average.

One of the benchmarks employed to assess the degree of reach of financial services to the population of the country, is the quantum of deposit accounts (current and savings) held as a ratio to the adult population. In the Indian context, taking into account the Census of 2001 (ignoring the incremental growth of population thereafter), the ratio of deposit accounts (data available as on March 31, 2004) to the total adult population was only 59 percent (details furnished in Table 9.2). Within the country, there is a wide variation across states. For instance, the ratio for the state of Kerala is as high as 89 percent while Bihar is marked by a low coverage of 33 percent. In the North Eastern States like Nagaland and Manipur, the coverage was a meagre 21 percent and 27 percent, respectively. The Northern Region, comprising the states of Haryana, Chandigarh and Delhi, has a high coverage ratio of 84 percent. Compared to the developed world, the coverage of our financial services is quite low.

A recent National Sample Survey revealed that out of 89 million farm households in India, more than 40 million households had no access to finance whether formal or informal. Out of the remaining 45 million households who had outstanding debt, more than 40 percent of this outstanding debt was from non-formal institutions such as moneylenders, etc. NSSO survey also showed that in recent years, the share of traditional system of credit such as moneylenders was probably on the rise in rural areas.

The All India Debt and Investment Survey 2002 revealed that the share of money lenders, which had declined from 69.7 percent in 1951 to 17.5 percent in 1991, has increased again to 27 percent by 2002 and that of non-institutional sources of credit has increased from 30 percent in 1991 to 39 percent in 2002. Thus while on one hand the number of banks and their branches and account holders is on the rise, non-formal credit sources are also creeping in which implies that the formal credit system has not been able to adequately penetrate the informal financial markets.

The distribution coverage of MFI and SHGs are skewed and concentrated in southern states of India. Since 1955 government of India has been taking efforts for inclusion such as creation of State Bank of India in 1955; nationalization of commercial banks in 1969 and 1980; initiating the Lead Bank Scheme in 1970; establishing Regional Rural Banks (RRBs) in 1975; introducing a Self-Help Group (SHG)-Bank Linkage Programme in 1992 and formulating the Kisan Credit Card scheme in 2001.

The common individual is deprived of access to banks for generating savings and for availing credit. This financial exclusion complicates day to day cash flow management, leads to inadequate financial planning and risk management and insecurity of old age. Lack of savings and saving avenues leads the population to avail the services of non-formal credit institutions.

Financial Inclusion Measures Till the End of 1990s

Realising that the rural population, which forms round 75 percent of our total population, needs simple, flexible and small-sized financial products in very large numbers, the Government set up the Regional Rural Banks (RRBs) in the mid seventies, which were visualized as hybrid banks incorporating the technical competency and professionalism of the Commercial Banks and the local feel and low cost structure of the cooperative credit system. Further, NABARD was established in 1982, as an apex level institution to deal with all issues related to agriculture and rural development. Thus, a multi-agency approach to address the needs of the poor was adopted. The impact of all these efforts resulted in extending the coverage of rural banking–there are over 32,000 rural bank branches of public and private sector banks and RRBs. The important milestones in the process of financial inclusion since independence are the following:

1954	-	Rural Credit Survey Committee.
1955	-	State Bank of India created for rural penetration.
1969	-	19 Commercial Banks nationalised; All India Rural Credit Review Committee.
1970	-	Lead Bank Scheme-States/Districts.
1975	-	Regional Rural Bank-Hybrid banks.
1981	-	6 more Commercial Banks nationalised.
1992	-	SHG-Bank Linkage Programme.

Financial Inclusion Measures in the New Millennium

The Reserve Bank of India recognized financial inclusion as thrust area and initiated a series of policy measures in recent years. The Bank's Annual Policy Statement for 2005-06, while recognising the concerns in regard to the banking practices that tend to exclude, rather than attract, vast sections of the population, urged banks to review their existing practices to align them with the objective of financial inclusion.

In 2006, the Government of India took some watershed steps for studying the issue of financial exclusion and devising strategic road map for financial inclusion for poor unbanked and under banked in India, consequent of which a commission headed by the eminent economist Dr. C. Rangarajan was formed and it came with its report on financial inclusion in 2008. The Report Committee on Financial Inclusion headed by Dr. C. Rangarajan (2008) stated that financial inclusion must be taken up in a mission mode and suggested a National Mission on Financial Inclusion (NMFI) comprising representation of all stakeholders for suggesting the overall policy changes required, and supporting stakeholders in the domain of public, private and NGO sectors in undertaking promotional initiatives. The report has come with some fundamental policy suggestions and chalking out new role play for existing and new institutions like Cooperatives, Banks, Regional Rural Banks, SHGs, JLGs, NBFCs and other financial intermediaries like BC and BF.

According to C. Rangarajan there are six approaches in the

system of Financial Inclusion:

1. Credit to the marginal and sub-marginal farmers and other small borrowers.
2. Extending the services of rural branches beyond providing credit to giving helping hand in terms of advice on a wide variety of matters relating to agriculture.
3. Opening new branches of commercial banks in districts where population per branch is much higher than the national average.
4. Simplification of the procedures in relation to granting of loans to small borrowers.
5. Strengthening the SHG-Bank Linkage Programme (BLP).
6. Effective implementation of the business facilitator and correspondent model.

Some important measures introduced since 2005 for financial inclusion are:

1. **No Frills Account:** The first measure in this direction, introduced in November 2005 was opening a basic banking "No Frills" Account with either nil or very minimum balances or charges that would make such accounts accessible to vast sections of the population. The required documents for no frill accounts are provided in regional language. Overdraft facility is extended on no frill account by various state banks. Know your customer (KYC) practice for account holder with balances not greater than ₹ 50,000 has been simplified. Ration card and voter ID are taken as KYC norms. Bio-metric cards are issued.
2. **General Purpose Credit Card (GCC) Facility:** The banks were advised to provide GCC facility at their rural and semi-urban branches for providing revolving credit to the cardholder to meet his financial requirements, up to ₹ 25,000. Overdue loans up to ₹ 25,000 are eligible for one time settlement. The borrowers availing one time settlement schemes are very much eligible for fresh loans.
3. **No White Spaces (NWS) Initiative of ICICI:** This

programme will cover 450 of 640 districts in rural India so that no individual will be more than 5 kms away from the ICICI touch point.

Intermediaries–From January 2006, banks were permitted to take assistance from Self-help groups, Micro Finance Institutions and other non-government organizations as business facilitators.

4. **Joint Liability Groups (JLGs):** A pilot project on financing Joint Liability Groups (JLG) was initiated for developing effective credit products for such clients who do not have the ability to provide adequate collateral security, which reduces risk and transaction costs for the banks and also introduce a greater degree of flexibility for the credit user to determine their credit needs and priorities.

   Joint Liability Groups (JLG), established under the project, comprise a group of 5-10 member clients who are together informally recognised by the bank as a group. The group members offer an undertaking to the bank that enables them to jointly receive such amounts as deemed eligible by the bank for pursuing any activity, individually or jointly, as found suitable by the group.
5. **Rythu Mitra Groups:** In Andhra Pradesh the programme called Rythu Mitra Groups envisages bringing about holistic development in the lives of small, marginal and landless farmers through collective action. RMGs are expected to serve as a conduit for technology transfer, facilitate access to market information and markets, assist in carrying out activities for modernizing farming. During 2005, 4437 RMGs were financed by 18 commercial banks, 9 RRBs and 9 DCCBs involving ground level credit flow of ₹ 28.11 crore. About 62,000 farmers have been assisted.
6. **Self-help Groups:** SHG-Bank Linkage programme aims at improving access of the weaker and other sections of the society from formal financial institutions. The ability of people to pool their micro-savings, provide collective

social collateral for banks to lend against and add to the SHGs' funds and the collective allocation of funds to meet emergent credit needs of the SHG members, charge rates which reflect risks and management cost of funds. This movement has enabled banks to assist in meeting the credit needs of very poor people without sacrificing their funds and has helped rural women especially to empower themselves both economically and financially. Over the last 20 years, the micro finance initiative of NABARD has assumed the shape of a micro finance movement in the country by linking around 74 lakh SHGs with the formal banking system by March 31, 2011. Further, the programme has enabled an estimated 10 crore poor households to gain access to funds.

7. **National Rural Financial Inclusion Plan (NRFIP):** Financial Inclusion Plan at the national level is being formulated by NABARD to provide access to comprehensive financial services to at least 50 percent (55.77 million) of the excluded rural cultivator and non-cultivator households, across different States by 2012 through rural/semi-urban branches of CBs and RRBs. The remaining households are targeted to be covered by 2015. It has been proposed that semi-urban and rural branches of commercial banks and RRBs may set for themselves a minimum target of covering 250 new cultivator and non-cultivator households per branch per annum, aggregating 11.15 mn. households p.a., with clear emphasis on financing marginal farmers, tenant cultivators and poor non-cultivator households. The national targets will be disaggregated State-wise with adequate focus on districts having a large percentage of population not accessing bank credit. To operationalise the NRFIP, DLCCs at district level shall draw up block-wise/village-wise maps of rural households not having access to formal credit sources. A State Level Rural Financial Inclusion Plan–SLRFIP is also proposed to be executed jointly by the State Level

Bankers' Committee (SLBC) and NABARD for arriving at a conclusive Financial Inclusion Plan for the State. With a minimum target coverage of 50 percent of currently excluded by the year 2012, States will be free to set for themselves higher targets.

8. **Financial Inclusion Funds:** Two funds may be constituted a Financial Inclusion Promotion and Development Fund, with NABARD, for meeting the cost of developmental and promotional interventions and a Financial Inclusion Technology Fund, with NABARD to meet the costs of technology adoption. Each Fund will have an initial corpus of ₹ 500 crore, with a start up funding of ₹ 250 crore each, to be contributed equally by GoI/RBI/NABARD and annual accretions thereto. Banks will be eligible for support from the Funds on a matching contribution of 50 percent from the Fund in regard to districts other than tribal districts and 75 percent in case of branches located in tribal districts identified under the Tribal Sub Plan. The second fund proposed is Financial Inclusion Technology Fund. For extending outreach on a scale envisaged under NRFIP would require the application of low-cost technology solutions, which call for certain levels of funding support for rolling out such IT-based and inclusive financial sector plan. NABARD, in consultation with RBI, may prepare detailed guidelines for operationalising the Funds.

9. **Others:** Nationwide Electronic Financial Inclusion System (NEFIS), Project Financial Literacy, Financial Literacy and Credit Counselling (FLCC) centres, and Financial Inclusion Technology Fund (FITF).

With ongoing efforts of financial inclusion the financial access points in India have been increased to reach out to the excluded. The number of 'no frills' accounts increased from 4,89,497 on 31st March 2006 to 41.5 Million as on June 30th, 2009. The lead bank in each district has been asked by RBI to draw a roadmap by the end of March 31, 2010 for ensuring that all villages with a population of over 2,000 will have access to financial services through a banking outlet, not necessarily a bank branch, by March 31, 2012.

Conclusion

Improvement in access to financial institutions affords several benefits to the consumer, regulator and the economy. It provides access to multi purpose, safe and standardized financial products that are regulated by credible regulators at low cost. Enhanced financial inclusion will drastically reduce the farmers' indebtedness which has been one of the main causes for farmer's suicides. It will result in increase in the rate of modernization of Indian agriculture. Newer activities which are gaining importance in the rural areas–horticulture, floriculture, organic farming, food processing etc. are cash intensive as they require improved seeds, fertilizers and other modern inputs and equipments. Enhanced financial inclusion, through better risk management tools for the farmers, will encourage farmers and small scale entrepreneurs to adopt new technologies at a faster rate. By providing greater access to educational loans to all sections of the society, improved financial inclusion will bring equal opportunities to the doorstep of each individual which is a pre-condition for achieving the goal of inclusive growth. Financial inclusion will promote grass root innovations and entrepreneurship by providing easily accessible micro-venture capital fund.

Solving the problem of financial exclusion requires a holistic approach on the part of the banks in creating awareness about financial products, education, and advice on money management, debt counselling, savings and affordable credit. The banks will have to evolve specific strategies to expand the outreach of their services in order to promote financial inclusion. Banks need to redesign their business strategies to incorporate specific plans to promote financial inclusion of low income group treating it both a business opportunity as well as a corporate social responsibility.

References

Dev, S Mahendra, October 14 2006. Financial Inclusion Issues and Challenges, Economic and Political Weekly.

GOI (2008), Report on the Committee on the Financial Inclusion, January 2008.

Kelakar V., 13 January 2008, Financial Inclusion for Inclusive Growth, N.P. Sen Memorial Lecture, ASC Hyderabad.

Mohan, R. 2002, Transforming Indian Banking in Search of a Better Tomorrow, RBI Bulletin January.

Mohan, R. 2004, Financial Sector Reforms in India: Policies and Performance Analysis, RBI Bulletin October.

Mohan, Rakesh, 2006, Economic Growth, Financial Deepening and Financial Inclusion, RBI Bulletin, November 2006.

Shri V.Leeladhar, 2 December 2005, Deputy Governor Reserve Bank of India Commemorative Lecture at the Fedbank Hormis Memorial Foundation at Ernakulam.

Subba Rao K. G. K (2007), Financial Inclusion: An Introspection, Economic and Political Weekly, Vol. 42, No. 05, February 03-February 09.

Thorat, Smt. Usha, June 19, 2007, Financial Inclusion – The Indian Experience. Text Speech at HMT-DFID Financial Inclusion Conference, Whitehall Place, London, UK, www.rbi.org–RBI speeches and reports RBI Bulletin, various issues.

5

Micro Finance for Rickshaw Pullers: A Case Study of Dibrugarh Town

Kumud Chandra Goswami

Introduction

Every one will agree that the rickshaw is environment friendly and most convenient mood of transport in the urban and semi urban areas. In every town and city, there are rickshaws plying on the road from the dawn to midnight to carry passengers and in some cases to carry goods. Generally, they remain waiting for the passengers at the places kept reserved for their parking in town area. There are rickshaws plying on the roads all over the globe. The pullers of this mode of transport are basically from the poor family background and uneducated or school drop outs. In India male are engaged in this profession of pulling rickshaws but in some foreign country it is the profession of the female. In Germany, females are involved in pulling rather driving rickshaws.

Rickshaws are relatively cheap and very handy for short-distance travel, where neither auto-rickshaw nor taxi drivers would agree to drop the passengers and goods. Although the rickshaws are very essential for a small town like Dibrugarh but the society is not very much concerned about the status of the pullers. The rickshaw pullers are unorganized and for this reason they have less bargaining powers to get their genuine demands fulfilled not to speak about their privileges. As a consequence, they are suffering a lot to earn their livelihood whatever they receive by carrying passengers and/or goods. In Dibrugarh Town, there are more than 1000 licensed rickshaws plying on the road and their number is increasing every year as per the Dibrugarh Town Municipality Board records.

However, in some routes there has been decline in the number of rickshaws because of introducing some auto rickshaws (Vikrams and Tempos) for carrying passengers within the town area. But the sound and dust created by these vehicles make the life of the dwellers of Dibrugarh Town very troublesome and painstaking. Cycle rickshaws are seen in almost every nook and corner of the country like India. Hand-pulled rickshaws have been a feature of Calcutta's streets for more than a century. And when one looks at the rickshaws closely we see great variation in their design and look. Some are narrow, some are wide, and a few have a covered top while at many places the top has been done away with. Ornamentation and decoration of the rickshaws also varies from region to region.

Rickshaw Pullers as Entrepreneurs

The paper has made an attempt to call the rickshaw pullers as entrepreneurs of a different status unlike the other entrepreneurs. The rickshaw pullers are running their enterprises without engaging any employee to help them out. Their enterprises mostly depend upon others support in the form of liquid resources or some resources in kinds i.e. taking the rickshaws (assets) on periodical rental mostly on daily rental basis. This category of entrepreneurs are doing entrepreneurial activities in an invisible way without having any permanency to the profession because in most cases their own investment is almost tends to zero and it requires hard labour. The entrepreneurs pulling rickshaw is earning form this profession taking the assets on lease basis and taking the risk of their earning. This type of entrepreneurs are most temporary in nature and at any time they may disappear but immediately another person takes over the work and the work remains in the system and continuously it is creating self employment. They are from the very poor family background and having inadequate educational qualification; mostly they are school drop out. They are mostly found in urban areas with a little bit presence in rural areas too. They are serving the society with the spirit of an entrepreneur. These entrepreneurs can also be termed as invisible entrepreneurs because they are least permanent.

A Brief Profile of Dibrugarh District

Dibrugarh district is located at north east corner of India. Some important statistics of the district have been shown in this paragraph. The district is also called green district as it is hosting a lot many tea gardens scattered over the entire district. Population in Dibrugarh District as per 2001 census was 11,85,072 with a male population of 6,13,555 and number of female was 5,71,517. Out of the population, 9.5 lakh live in villages and the urban population was about 2.3 lakh. The literacy rate of the district was 58.91 percent. Geographical area of the district is 3381 sq. km. with three towns, 144 numbers of tea gardens, 14 colleges, one medical college, one university so it can be said that the district is economically rich and also have a good educational infrastructure although the literacy rate is below 60 percent. Dibrugarh Town is the district head quarter and as such a considerable number of people from other areas of the district happens to come for various purposes. The town is expanding at a very high speed because of the new bridge over the river Brahmaputra is coming up and a gas cracker project is going to establish nearby the Dibrugarh Town. These two big projects increase the importance of the town. There is enough scope for tea tourism, river tourism and nature tourism but these are not yet explored to attract tourist from outside.

This study has been made to fulfil the following objectives:

1. To know the ownership pattern of rickshaws plying on the road of Dibrugarh Town.
2. To examine the entrepreneurial activity of the rickshaw pullers.
3. To study the economic condition of the rickshaw pullers

and the financing pattern of them in the study area.

4. To suggest some ways and means to improve the economic status of the rickshaw pullers by giving a new look on them.

The entire study is based on observation made by the researcher as such no technical tools have been used. The study has been conducted on 50 rickshaw pullers in the Dibrugarh Town out of the total approximate population of 1000 rickshaw pullers as per the municipal authority records as on 31st March, 2010. Out of the total population a considerable number of rickshaws are not plying on the road for various reasons. So, it is very difficult to ascertain the exact number of rickshaws that are plying on the road in Dibrugarh Town on regular basis. However, on an average 600-700 rickshaws are regularly plying on the road. From the population, we have selected 50 rickshaw pullers as sample as per convenience of the researcher. The survey has been made in the first week of August, 2010 over three to four days.

The sample population has been interviewed with the help of a schedule and observation has been made on the basis of data generated after interviewing them. The sample respondents are not educated enough so the researcher has asked them questions in their vernacular languages as they are not in a position to understand the English language. The analysis has been made on the basis of some simple analytical tools and inferences have been made on the basis of such analysis. The researcher has referred some literature available in soft form from various web sites as no such literature in hard form is available on rickshaw pullers.

The study has been conducted taking a very small sample from the total population; had the sample size been large the findings would have been more authentic. In our study area we have seen that almost all the rickshaw pullers are from very poor family background, most of them are not having their own rickshaw, their working time is also identical and as such their other problems are also expected to be more identical.

Therefore, we cannot expect most significant difference in findings by increasing the size of the sample. Another problem the researcher has faced when the project was undertaken is the non-availability of literature about the rickshaw pullers both at the national and international levels. As a result, our reference is very short. Formal and extensive research work on the rickshaw pullers has perhaps not yet been made what we have observed when the researcher has searched for literature in this area both in soft and hard form. As such, the researcher could not provide much in the bibliography at the end of paper.

Family Background and Status of the Rickshaw Pullers

A major portion of the rickshaw pullers are from rural areas surrounding Dibrugarh town, some are migrated from other districts, and some of them also migrated from other states of India. We have met a considerable number of rickshaw pullers who has migrated from Dhemaji District located in the north bank of Brahmaputra river. They come to Dibrugarh in search of jobs because many of them have lost their agricultural land in flood which has been their primary source of income. Since they lost everything in natural disaster and finding no other alternative sources of income they rushed to Dibrugarh Town in search of some engagement so that they can maintain their family. They are mostly school dropout after studying up to class VI or VII they could not study further for poor economic condition and in some cases for lack of guidance from their parents and other well wishers. Although they are literate but with their level of education they could not enter into other jobs and ultimately they joined in this profession.

It has been observed that out of the total sample respondents twenty four are not having any formal education and four has passed HSLC examination and the others are school dropout. It appears that most of the rickshaw pullers are having some education so there is scope to train them up to make them more successful in this profession. We have also asked them one question regarding their number of dependent family members and we have observed that they are not over burdened with the number family who are dependent upon them. Out of the sample respondents 48 rickshaw pullers are married and having 1 to 3 children and rest are unmarried but they are to maintain their parents and sisters and brothers with their hard earned money. The married person are managing their micro family and normally they need not face much financial hardship as they are earning moderately but when any family member falls sick they suffer a lot because of higher medical expenditure.

Income and Saving Habits of Rickshaw Pullers

With some hesitation we have asked the rickshaw pullers questions to enquire about their income level. When we asked them about their level of income we have surprised that they do not hesitate in sharing their information about income. It signifies that they are very simple citizen and they are more transparent in disclosing a little bit personal information. The earning size of the rickshaw pullers are shown in Table 10.1 After interacting with them we have come to know that their earning varies in between ₹ 80 to ₹ 200 per day. Of the total sample 40 percent (20) says that they are earning in between ₹ 120 to ₹ 140 daily and 24 percent (12) rickshaw pullers say that they are earning ₹ 80 to ₹ 100 and 20 percent (10) of them says that their earning ranges from ₹ 100 to ₹ 120. It appears that (Table 5.1) the rickshaw pullers earning is not very meagre.

When we have asked the pullers about their savings behaviour then we have got a positive signal on them. After meeting their daily requirements they are in a position to save something for their future needs as well as for investment. Table 5.2 has highlighted the savings pattern of the rickshaw pullers. From the table we have seen that out of 50 rickshaw pullers only 24 (48 percent) are saving in public institutions and the rest 52 percent do not save.

Table 5.1: Daily Income of the Sample Rickshaw Pullers

Daily income (Rs.)	No. of rickshaw Pullers
80- 100	12 (24)
100-120	10 (20)
120-140	20 (40)
140-170	4 (8)
170-180	2 (4)
180-200	2 (4)
Total	50 (100)

Figures in brackets indicate percentage (percent).
Source: Field Survey.

From among the savers 8 (33.33 percent) of them save in post offices, 6 (25 percent) are investing in banks and 10 (41.67 percent) select Sahara as their first choice. Those who are not involved in savings they say that they are not in a position to save out of their earning but it seem to be not the real situation. From informal talk with them we have come to know that those who do not save are casual and some are habitual alcoholic. They need some sorts of counselling for savings and to bring them out from the habit of consuming alcohol.

Table 5.2: Savings Pattern of the Rickshaw Pullers

Savings p.m.	Total no. of savers	No. of savers in post office	No. of savers in banks	No. of savers in Sahara
Less than ₹ 100	0	0	0	0
Between ₹ 100-200	2	2	0	0
Between ₹ 200-300	8	4	2	2
Between ₹ 300-400	8	0	0	8
Between ₹ 400-500	4	0	4	0
Between ₹ 500 and above	2	2	0	0

Source: Field Survey.

We have also asked them questions relating to their expenses for running and maintenance of their vehicles. They say that normally they spent ₹ 30-40 per month and those who are running others vehicle it goes from the pocket of the pullers but when the expenses cross ₹ 300 then it is to be spent by the vehicle owners. This is almost common for all the landlords providing vehicles on daily rental basis.

It has been observed that the rickshaw pullers are having the capacity of taking risk volatile income pattern and to bear the rental to be paid to the rickshaw owner and to maintain the vehicle at their own cost. They are hard workers and their income depends upon number of users and distance they can cover in a day. They also think to have their own vehicle and some of them become successful.

Ownership Pattern of the Rickshaws

The cycle rickshaws plying on the road are not owned by the pullers in many cases. They cannot afford to have their own rickshaw because it costs ranges from ₹ 6,000 to ₹ 8,000 in the present market. From the sample respondents we have found that 22 rickshaw pullers are driving their own vehicles and the rest 28 are running rickshaws owned by the landlord and they are to pay ₹ 20 per day to the landlord as royalty and in case of a new vehicle this royalty rate is ₹ 30 daily. We have found one rickshaw puller who owned three rickshaws and still he is engaged in this profession. He is in real sense an entrepreneur who is taking the risk of engaging himself in this profession although he is having some other sources of income.

He took bank loan when he purchased his first rickshaw then he is not looking back and is making money and growing richer day by day. In this regard the micro finance institutions can come forward to help these people by providing loans and other assistance as and when required on easy terms and conditions. There is scope to form a specialized institution to finance the rickshaws only to those who will be directly involved in the rickshaw pulling profession. The success story of the Self Employed Women's Association (SEWA) promoted SEWA Bank (Shri Mahila SEWA Sahakari Bank Ltd.) from Gujarat State can be cited not only here in Dibrugarh but also in other places. In Assam, there has been a rickshaw bank project run by Centre for Rural Development (CRD) a registered NGO giving opportunity to the rickshaw pullers to have their own rickshaw by paying daily instalment. This rickshaw bank is helping the rickshaw-entrepreneurs by nurturing their zeal to be in this profession but it is not yet coming to the town under study.

It needs to form an association of the rickshaw pullers. In this respect some help from NGOs or other expert may be sought for. Ex- bank official with some dedication to work and to help the down trodden people can take a lead to help these entrepreneurs like the rickshaw pullers and the street vendors who need very meagre amount of loan comparatively for a short span of time. If this comes to a reality then this profession will come up in a big way in small town like Dibrugarh. The cycle rickshaws not only will create some direct employment but also lot of indirect job avenues will also come up in due course. A rickshaw bank can be opened to look after the interest of the rickshaw pullers. Such a bank can enter into area like generating savings amongst the pullers, providing loan both productive as well as consumption loan when they could not earn sufficient to maintain their family, providing insurance services, creating a financial base for their old age support and many more welfare activities.

Working Time and Fare Charged by the Rickshaw Pullers

All the rickshaw pullers keep themselves ready to work from 7.00 A.M. to 7.00 P.M. generally with some break for lunch in the afternoon session. Out of total sample population 32 of them works in normal time. We met 18 rickshaw pullers who started their work late night and continue till morning (from about 2.00 A.M. to 10.00 A.M.) and in the evening session they again drive their vehicles. They select this odd time to earn more fares then fares they charge from the day time passengers. They have shared with the information that for early morning and late night services they charge fares more than double to that of normal rate of fare.

There is a system of fixing fares for the rickshaws by the local municipality authority on km. basis so that the pullers cannot charge more and harass the passengers in the name of charging fares from them. But one problem we have seen that the fares to be charged are displayed neither in the vehicles nor at the place meant for their parking creating hardship to the commuters in paying fares. The travellers from outside Dibrugarh face a lot of problems in paying rickshaw fares because of lack of transparency in the fare rates. In this respect the local authority must pay adequate attention to help the commuters and the rickshaw pullers too so that this service can be expanded by making it more user friendly. In the course of undertaking this project we have met 6 rickshaw pullers from among the sample respondents and we have come to know that very now and then they engaged themselves in some of their traditional works like agricultural at their native place. This indicates that all the rickshaw pullers are not full time worker in this profession. This gives an indication that the entrepreneurial spirit of the rickshaw pullers have not yet been coming up. The existing pullers need some sort of training how to behave with the passengers, how to communicate with others so that they can remain in this profession and can maintain and improve their earning level.

Social Dignity of the Rickshaw Pullers

Since the rickshaws are slow moving vehicle runs manually it creates traffic congestions on road in rush hours especially in the morning and in the evening hours. The rickshaw pullers at that moment get rough behaviour from all sections of the society. The members of the society those who are not regular commuter of this type of vehicle feel that the rickshaws should be removed from the road then the traffic congestion will be reduced. The rickshaw pullers in some situation become the victims of physical torture from the members of the society. The police personnel also do some sorts of harassment upon them not for any very serious causes. In some cases the police personnel torture them physically, seize their vehicles and try to take something from them as official fines and in some cases unofficial fines too. The rickshaw pullers say that most of the passengers they carry are very kind to them and try to compensate them by giving justified fares. But there are some passengers who unnecessarily argue for fares and they misbehave the rickshaw pullers. Public awareness about the hard labour made by the rickshaw pullers is very less as a result they are not getting proper behaviour from the member of the society.

The rickshaw pullers are required to come forward to serve the society through their dedicated service. Both the people and the pullers must create a situation which helps both of them and the riding will also be comfortable and hassle free all the way. To make the service more comfortable the pullers have to fulfil certain standards of their services. Some of such things that will not cost the pullers are maintaining their dress code during their working hours, obeying traffic signals and other rules on the roads, maintaining cordial relationship with the passengers and the public in general and the administrative machinery. The members of the society should properly understand the dignity of labour of the rickshaw pullers and should encourage them. There are something more to be done by experts like redesigning the vehicle to make it more comfortable in driving and also for the commuters. With upgraded gears, hydraulic brakes, rear end differential, comfortable seats, halogen lights, the cycle rickshaw which today covers a distance of 60 km. per day on an average, can emerge as one of the most efficient non-motorised transport in the cities.

The ban on rickshaw pulling has come as a setback for the

rickshaw pullers who have been serving the commuters. But this is not the solution to the problems created by the rickshaws in urban areas. This is the only public mode of non-motorised transport facility available in the ever changing world. So it is high time to think and to retain the service rather improve it for the interest of the future generations of the human society. The rickshaw pullers are not having any common platform for their collective bargaining although most of them are dedicated to their profession. One rickshaw puller says that during summer when the mercury goes past 40C people hate to being anywhere near the sun.

However, despite the sweltering heat, they carry out their duties, providing comfort to fellow human beings. In spite of this sort of dedication of the rickshaw pullers if the commuters cannot feel the problems and the working condition in paying fares to the rickshaw pullers then they will not be able to provide the required level of service. Now time has come to think collectively by all the rickshaw pullers to protect their interest and to take the challenges coming from the faster mood of travel and also changing mind set of the urban people towards this mood of transport. Few organisations of social activists and some urban dwellers argue that the rickshaws should be removed from the road as it creates lot of problems to the faster mood of transport and there has been frequent collision between car owners and the rickshaw pullers. But the question is: where will these needy members of the society go once they have been deprived of something they have been doing so efficiently for years?

Problem of Resources of Rickshaw Pullers

Let us take a hypothetical example for the benefit of the rickshaw pullers. At least 50 pullers can form a group in the style of cooperative may be registered or may remain unregistered as per their understanding. Each member will contribute ₹ 5 per day; means total collection per day will be ₹ 250 i.e. (5x50) to be deposited into a bank according to the convenience of the members in the name of the society not in the name of any individual. Continuing this saving pattern for one month they will be able to accumulate Rs. 7,500 i.e. (250x30) and that too without interest (for simplification we have ignored interest element). The study has also revealed that the rickshaw pullers save money in various banks and post offices; therefore, to save another ₹ 5 per day will not create any financial problem on them.

With this accumulation in the hands of the cooperative they will be able to purchase one rickshaw every month as property of their cooperative and the same is to be given to a member who is not driving his own vehicle may be on the basis of lottery or according to their mutual understanding when the number of member not having their own vehicle is more than one. The member who will drive vehicle of the cooperative will pay rent for that ₹ 10 on daily basis (i.e. less than the rent charged by the landlord) this provision will generate some income of the cooperative in the near future. The income of the cooperative means the income of the members as they will get their share in due course when the cooperative grows satisfactorily. In the initial years, the cooperative should not distribute any dividend.

If every month one rickshaw is purchased by the cooperative then over less than 50 months all the members will be able to have their own vehicle. In the initial years whatever being realized from the rental income by the cooperative can be spent to meet its recurring expenses. Gradually, the income from rental will go on increasing when there is increase in the number of rickshaws. Once all the members get their own rickshaw, the cooperative can start giving financial help (loan) to the members at some nominal interest to be repaid in a limited period. The cooperative will sanction and disburse loan to the members for genuine cause and in some cases may be even a consumption loan. This system will help the members to phase out the debt trap situation being faced by them. Some genuine NGO who are really working for the society may help the rickshaw pullers to promote this concept of financing this type of very small project.

To attract tourist or visitors to enjoy rickshaw riding the pullers should be trained up regarding how to deal with the passengers so that both the pullers and the commuters can maximize their satisfaction. In this regard the pullers may be given a license along with a dress code to be used at the time of their duty period. In Puri (Orissa), the process is going on for the benefit of the tourist because Puri is a famous tourist place. To help the rickshaw pullers in Puri (Orissa) some NGOs has initiated some training programmes. One rickshaw puller has given his observation about the said training programme. "I enjoy these training sessions. It is a different kind of experience for rickshaw pullers like us. I hope my standard of living will improve after this training," said Pramod Pattnaik,a rickshaw puller. Another rickshaw puller has said that "Lack of support had made our lives wretched. We are glad to receive guidance in making our lives better," another rickshaw puller Loknath Reddy said.

Although, in Dibrugarh, there is scope for developing tourism but it is not yet coming up. To attract the tourist a new concept may be taken up i.e. “Rickshaw Tourism” which is not yet coming up any where in the world. But this need a lot of home work on the part of the administration and other social organization. First thing we have to renovate the rickshaws plying on our roads to make it comfortable for the passengers and the pullers. New rickshaw designs are coming up in many countries. Some of such new designs can be operated by electric battery and some can be operated by solar power. Introducing these new designs in Dibrugarh Town the neglected profession can be made more prestigious and challenging to the entrepreneurs.

To make the rickshaw service more popular among the new generation now and then race can be arranged among the pullers and other public as well. This new idea may boost up the moral of the pullers. This profession needs some more entrepreneurial touch so that the service can be sold in the competitive market.

Conclusion

We have seen that all the rickshaw pullers are not economically deprived. Their earning is more or less moderate. But economic progress of the rickshaw pullers will be possible by giving them counselling on forming a group/ cooperative for their common benefits. If such a group can do the work with a clean mind then it can be expected that it will be a financial institution owned by a group for the benefit of the group members and gradually they will be able to help the other section of the society specially other entrepreneurs in some other field.

References

Nining Sri Asututi Soesilo: The Role of Micro Finance and Micro Entrepreneur in Poverty Eradication Efforts in Indonesia.

Report of the Reserve Bank of India. Committee on Informal Financial Sector Statistics with Professor P. Venkataramiah as Chairman.

6

Agricultural Subsidies and Food Security in India under WTO Regime

Sakeer E. and Rais Ahmad

This paper examines the state of food security in India, based on an analysis of a selection of indicators of food security and nutritional wellbeing during the period 1995-2011 within the context of the WTO Agreements. Ensuring food security that is the access of the population to sufficient food to meet its nutritional requirements is a basic objective of governmental policies in agrarian developing countries like India. Hence, food security issues cover not only issues related to the availability and stability of food supplies but also to issues of access to this supply i.e., related to the resources that may be needed to procure the required quantity of food.

Attempt has been made to identify how a future multilateral agreement on agricultural trade can provide a secure framework within which India can pursue effective policies to ensure their food security. Rising incomes, urbanization, and shifting consumption patterns have increased food consumption in many areas of the world. According to the Millennium Ecosystem Assessment, the prospect of providing sufficient food to sustain another 2 billion people by 2020 has rightly focused attention on the very real threats to food security if the productivity of agricultural systems cannot keep pace with this demand. As these systems are under increasing pressure to meet the growing need for food, it is also vital that the environmental challenges associated with food production are addressed effectively–water pollution, pesticide use, land degradation and greenhouse gas emissions, amongst others (ICTSD, 2009). Since 2008, a large number of governments have shown markedly more interest in the question of how to manage volatility in global commodity markets, and how to protect people from escalating food costs (Sophia, 2010).

Food security in India is essential to maintain and sustain the food security system and ensure a safety net for the poor.

In many countries, health problems related to dietary excess are an ever increasing threat, In fact, malnutrition and food borne diarrhoea are become double burden. Agriculture remains the largest employment sector in most developing countries and international agriculture agreements are crucial to a country's food security. Some critics argue that trade liberalization may reduce a country's food security by reducing agricultural employment levels. Concern about this has led a group of World Trade Organization (WTO) member states to recommend that current negotiations on agricultural agreements allow developing countries to re-evaluate and raise tariffs on key products to protect national food security and employment. They argue that WTO agreements, by pushing for the liberalization of crucial markets, are threatening the food security of whole communities.

By 2050, the world's population will stabilize at about 9 billion, but because of increasing consumption in developing countries, it will be equivalent to 12 billion people placing demands on the global food system, compared to today's consumption rates. Given currently available technologies, current consumption patterns, and the negative effects of climate change, food security for all cannot be achieved. According to IFPRI research, the current recession and the corresponding reduced investment in the global economy will lead to an increase in agricultural prices in the medium term, with the number of hungry (Joachim, 2009).

The aggregate impact of changes in trade policy on the food security of a particular country would depend on the relevant strategy pursued: food self-reliance or food self-sufficiency. Self-reliance in food is when a country pursues an externally oriented trade regime with a view to earning enough from its exports of goods and services to finance its food requirements. On the other hand, the food self-sufficiency approach entails the country meeting its food requirements—or a substantial part of it—from domestic production (Samuel, 2006).

But economists argue that trade liberalization should enhance food security, enabling imports to offset production shortages. The purpose of this research is to determine how the Indian governments address long-run chronic and short-run acute food insecurity, and whether that has changed as a result of the considerable trade liberalization already undertaken by developing country food importers, largely due to conditionality of structural adjustment programs. Lessons will also be drawn for the design of future trade policy reforms that could further impact food security. Ever since India became a signatory to the WTO Agreement on Agriculture (AoA) in 1995, a concern that has been raised repeatedly is whether agricultural trade liberalization would destroy India's food security.

What is Food Security?

Food Security as defined by FAO is the physical and economic access for all people at all times to enough food for an active, healthy life with no risk of losing such access and as such is directly connected with livelihood in the developing countries. The World Food Summit of 1996 defined food security as existing "when all people at all times have access to sufficient, safe, nutritious food to maintain a healthy and active life". Commonly, the concept of food security is defined as including both physical and economic access to food that meets people's dietary needs as well as their food preferences. Food (in) security is primarily a phenomenon relating to individuals, and is determined by three sets of factors concerned with supply, access and guarantees to food (Christopher).

In most developing countries, an important determinant of

food security is food production. This is because most of the food-insecure people live in rural areas, earn a substantial share of their income from agriculture, and meet a significant share of their food requirements directly from their own food production (Salih, 1994).

Food security, trade liberalisation and the World Trade Organisation (WTO) have all been at the centre of various public and expert debates, amongst academicians, policy makers, in the media and in the civil society at large, both at national and international levels. Quite often, the various views expressed in these debates start from widely differing premise, even different notions of what constitutes food security, its links to international trade, the role of WTO in influencing food security, and so on.

According to P.V Srinivasan "Food security implies access by all people at all times to sufficient quantities of food to lead and active and healthy life". This requires not just adequate supply of food at aggregate level but also enough purchasing capacity with the individual/household to demand adequate levels of food. As far as the question of "enough purchasing capacity" is concerned, it involves the introduction of employment generation programmes, so that the income and purchasing power of the people increases.

As far as the question of "adequate supply" is concerned, it involves two dimension: 1. The Quantitative Dimension (in the sense that the over all food availability in the economy should be sufficient to meet the demand), and 2. The Qualitative Dimension (in the sense that the nutritional requirement of the pollution are properly looked after).

The Quantitative Aspects

Because of chronic food shortage that the country faced in the years following independence, the focus of food policy was to achieve self sufficiency. This has enabled the economy to overcome the problems of food grains shortages and build up large stocks of food grains to counter any scarcity condition. In fact, as noted by R Radhakrishnan, India achieved self-sufficiency in food grains in 1970s and as sustained it since then. It improved its capacity to cope with year-to-year fluctuations in food production by building up large buffer stocks though the agency of FCI (Food Corporation of India) and supplying these stocks to the people through the PDS.

The Qualitative Aspects

Even more worrisome is the qualitative aspects of the problem as the following facts clearly bring out.

1. According to the World Food Programme, nearly 50 percent of the World's hungry live in India.
2. About 35 percent of India's Population, over 350 million is food-insecure, consuming less than 80 percent of minimum energy requirement.
3. Nearly 9 out of 10 pregnant women between 15 and 49 years are mal-nourished and anaemic.
4. Malnutrition accounts for 50 percent of under-5 deaths.
5. Percentage of children suffering from anaemia is 77. In other words, 3 out of 4 children in India are anaemic.
6. Percentage of stunted children is 37 i.e. one out of three children has stunted growth.
7. Percentage of children not fully immunised is 51.

To tackle the qualitative and quantitative aspects of the food security problem, the government of India has relied on the food-based safety net.

Food Insecurity in India and WTO

Harmony with nature, and the expression of gratefulness to mother earth for bestowing on us the fruits of our labour nurturing her, constitutes the core elements of the agrarian tradition in India. Many developing countries including India fear that with trade liberalization they have given up tools to address both chronic and acute food insecurity. Hence, food security is prominent in their WTO negotiating positions on agriculture. In India, this is a critical issue since a large section of the population is dependent on agriculture for their livelihood, and the poor consumers already spend an overwhelming share of their income on food (Hoda et al., 2002).

India, with a billion plus population, has put agriculture at the heart of its economy and food security at the centre of its agriculture policy (Vandana, 2004). However, all the decisions and policies of a free and independent India which replaced colonial policies of land alienation, and concentration on ownership of land, super exploitation of the peasantry, the creation of famines are being undone through globalization and WTO agreements (Vandana, 2004).

For large agrarian developing countries like India, food security is an important and integral element of national security. Physical access to food in developing countries can be ensured only through a certain minimum level of self-sufficiency. Further, the subsistence and livelihood of farmers in large agrarian economies can also be seriously jeopardised due to cheap/subsidised imports. Other factors like the limitations of developing country farmers to change to other crops or to shift from agriculture to manufacturing or services, and the inability of developing countries to set apart required foreign exchange resources for making purchases from the volatile global markets, as also the difficulties in ensuring timely distribution of imported food grains to remote and backward areas are also significant issues in safeguarding the food security and livelihood in these countries.

Indian agriculture is unique because it has to meet the needs of over 1 billion people as well as provide liveable wages and income to nearly 600 million of its employees. The former is well reflected in India's share of global commodity production. For example, in 2006, India was the world's second largest producer of rice, sugar, milk and cotton, and third largest producer of wheat. Despite production volumes, food shortages and price inflation can destabilize the political environment and hence, food security and price stability are important policy objectives. Since agriculture is the major source of income to a large share of the Indian population, any structural adjustment arising from external sources is of serious concern to Indian policymakers (Munisamy, 2008).

Several commodities like wheat, coarse grains, oilseeds, vegetable oils, sugar, dairy products, fruits and vegetable which are of great significance for food security in developing countries have been subjected to high levels of export subsidies by the developed countries. By artificially depressing the international prices, these subsidies in developed countries lower the farm incomes of otherwise efficient producers in importing countries and thus adversely affect their livelihood. It is in this context of high trade distortions being practised in developed countries that the developing country members would require an appropriate level of tariff protection. As such, any reduction in tariffs by the developing countries could be considered only after substantial reduction in trade distorting domestic subsidies and elimination of export subsidies (Ministry of Commerce and Industry, 2001).

Rice is a primary staple food in India, can ill afford to depend on national market for meeting their food security needs. Though free trade can go a long way towards meeting food security needs of countries deficient in food grain production it cannot be relied upon as a safe option particularly in times of war. For, in times of war food may be used as a blackmailing weapon by enemy States to demoralize the country engaged in war. Apart from that, a country may not have adequate foreign currency reserves to finance import of food grains. Food security cannot be left to the mercy of free trade mechanism by countries where primary staple food is rice. It is because tradable surplus of rice in world market is not enough to take care of food security needs of even one country with sizable population. For example, total consumption of rice in 1998 in Malaysia was around 30 million tonnes while the amount of rice trade that year in international market was just around 20 million tonnes. The tradable surplus in world rice market cannot take care of a 210 million strong population of Indonesia, let alone India with population over 1 billion. The food security concerns of Member States are also echoed in the preamble to the Agreement on Agriculture.

The food security in India is facing the problems of both controlled and uncontrolled marketing deficiencies. Unless that sector is sustainable you cannot really look for options for people to achieve food security in the immediate short or even mid-term. Unfortunately, in the past, the food security issue was delinked from agricultural production. Around 35 percent world's food insecure population lives in India and 10-15 percent of the total households in India are food insecure, and do not get an assurance of getting at least two meals a day. Though PDS is a major step in bringing the food security clause into the mainstream, many of the states does not get the proper support from the State itself. There are problems of health and education access because of the increasing expenses incurred on costly food. Landlessness and the casualisation of labour have grown, and the seasonality of rural work has sharpened every decade, every year.

Agricultural Subsidies

The issue of agricultural subsidies is a highly politically sensitive issue. The food security in India is essential to maintain and sustain that food security and ensure a safety net for the poor. Subsidies on agricultural inputs such as irrigation, power and fertilizers are necessary to enable the poor and marginal farmers to have access to them. If agricultural inputs are not subsidized, the poor farmers will not be able to use them and this will lead to a decline in their income and productivity levels. But the benefits of subsidies on agricultural inputs are mostly concerned by large farmers and industry while small and marginal farmers fail to derive much gain. Continuation of agricultural subsidies is against the spirit of the AoA as adopted by the WTO and, in any case, such subsidies have to be reduced in accordance with commitments made by the member countries to the WTO.

The level of support provided by the developed countries to their agriculture is much higher as compared with developing countries and that the former have cleverly drafted the AoA in such a way as to derive maximum benefits from the phased reduction in agricultural subsides by the latter while at the same time ensuring that their own agriculture continues to be adequately protected from the export of the developing countries. Therefore the issue of agricultural subsidies is not to be examined only from the point of view of fiscal unsustainability but from a much wider perspective of ensuring food security and safety net for the poor and protecting the interests of the country in the new emerging international economic order that is taking shape under the aegis of the WTO.

Trade liberalisation and globalization of agriculture is robbing the peasants and landless workers of already low incomes and livelihood security. There are three mechanisms by which the rural producers are either being super-exploited or they are being rendered dispensable.

1. Destruction of the market support at domestic level both in terms of procurement and in terms of guarantee of Minimum Support Price (MSP). The MSP is to agriculture what minimum wages are in the individual and service sectors, the minimum prices a farmer should receive to cover costs of production and her/his labour. However, as a result of globalization, the government has started to withdraw from its role in procurement and price regulation. Riots have occurred in different parts of the country with farmers protesting against lack of markets and fall in prices of agricultural commodities.
2. Diversion from food crops to perishable cash crops and promotion of monocultures thus creating market dependency on corporate monopolies. Globalization policies have promoted the idea that farmers should shift

from food grains and stapes to vegetables and fruits. Export promotion zones for fruits and vegetables are a major thrust area in the new agriculture policy. On the one hand this erodes food security for households and the nation. On the other hand it pushes farmers into distress sales, since fruits and vegetables cannot be consumed or stored at the household level.

3. Removal of Quantitative Restrictions (QRs) on imports and dumping of subsidized, artificially cheap imports. A dispute initiated by the U.S. against India in the WTO forced the removal of QRs. This has translated into destruction of domestic markets and prices in India being perturbed by the artificially low international prices of commodities. While forcing India to remove import restrictions and reduce domestic support to farmers and the poor, the US has further increased its farm subsidies to US$ 180 billion over the next six years amounting to US$ 20 billion annually. Most of these subsidies go to agribusiness and to capture export markets. In addition, US$ 10 million funding was made available for export promotions by 65 U.S. trade organizations under the 2002 Market Access Program (MAP) and another US$ 90 million for Market Access under the fiscal year 2002. The Farm Bill 2002 also provides that MAP funding be increased to US$ 200 million by 2006.

Transnational agribusiness giants like Cargill, ADM and Conagra are, in fact, the only beneficiaries from the liberalization of imports and removal of import restrictions. They benefit both from using their immense financial clout to depress world prices during procurement and hike it during sales, as well as from the various subsidies that are given to them for both exporting as well as importing, from both exporting and importing countries. A recently released report from the International Agriculture and Trade Policy Institute has shown that in four major U.S. commodities, the level of dumping has increased since 1995 when the WTO came into force, even though the proclaimed aim of WTO is to "reduce distortions in trade". From 1995-2001 dumping jumped from 23-44 percent in the case of wheat, 9-29 percent in the case of soyabeans, 11-33 percent in the case of maize, and from 17-57 percent in the case of cotton. According to the World Bank, low cotton prices in U.S. resulting from high subsidies are costing African countries US$ 250 million each year (Vandana, 2003).

Food Security in India: Role of WTO

The Uruguay Round Agreement on Agriculture mentions food security as a legitimate "non-trade" concern of agricultural policy, but the agreement focused exclusively on liberalizing trade in agricultural products.

WTO members have constantly been confirming their commitment to the objective of sustainable development. They all are convinced that the aims of upholding and safeguarding an open and non-discriminatory multilateral trading system and acting for the protection of the environment and the promotion of sustainable development can and must be mutually supportive (Anil, 2004). S&DT related to rural development and food security was also specifically identified as an objective of the agriculture negotiations in the Doha Declaration.

However, here I think results from WTO to Indian food security have a negative impact. There are three dimensions- ecological security; livelihood security and food security are essential elements of an agriculture policy which is sustainable and equitable. Sustainable agriculture is based on sustainable use of natural resources—land, water and agricultural biodiversity (including plants and animals). The current globalization processes of agriculture through WTO threaten to undermine all three dimensions of agriculture policy. They are undermining ecological security by removing all limits on concentration of ownership of natural resources—land, water and biodiversity, and encouraging non-sustainable resource exploitation for short- term profits. The WTO agreement on agriculture combined with TRIPS agreement implies total monopoly over agriculture by a handful on global corporations, and total vulnerability of farmers to crop failure and indebtedness (Chandra, 2004).

Role of TRIPS in Food Security in India

Another WTO agreement–TRIPS–also affects human rights in agriculture, because it makes it mandatory for countries to provide patent protection for micro-organisms, non-biological and micro-biological processes as well as providing protection for plant varieties either by patents, or by an "effective sui generis system." The fear of such a system of patent protection on genetic resources for food and agriculture is that it could raise the cost of seed and agricultural inputs making them unaffordable for small-scale farmers in developing countries. Another problem is that TRIPS allows patenting of the shared knowledge of indigenous communities. The patenting of seeds coupled with technologies such as "terminator" technology could have drastic effects on the human rights of farmers in India. Farmers are committing suicides, reports of starvation deaths have become common, foreboding a return of famines last experienced under British rule. This chapter examines these developments in detail and proposes an agenda for creating an alternative future of food and highlights the current practices that are working towards this alternative.

Further, globalization of agricultural trade poses a great challenge to the future world food security. The control of seeds and agricultural research in a handful of MNCs–Gene Giants–Monsanto, DuPont and Syngenta, not only renders the food security of the world vulnerable in the hands of these commercial enterprises but may also tend to affect the quality and well-being of everyone with food habits totally dictated by the MNCs to appease their "hunger for corporate wealth and power". The rich nations are adopting any and every type of means–fair or foul, to protect their farmers. Farmers in the LDCs, whose very economic survival depends on being able to save seeds from one year to the next, are ruined by added input costs. Ironically, the community which helped MNCs develop the new varieties of crops are not only denied ownership rights but are also made to pay royalties for use of their own resources. Apart from the need to purchase seeds every year, they perforce have to use chemical herbicides and fertilizers. Uniformity in plant varieties and mono-cropping world over may also affect the gene pool, perhaps, irreversibly, besides rendering food security totally dependent upon the stability of the international seed supply industry (Lalitha et al., 2006).

Role of AoA in Food Security in India

I feel that at this juncture it is important to closely examine this aspect of the AoA, so as to ensure that the reform process in the agriculture sector takes into consideration the food security and other non-trade concerns of countries like India. At the same time, as indicated in the preamble, the AoA recognized non-trade concerns (NTCs) of countries. These NTCs included food security and the need to protect the environment.

AoA addresses food security issues. The trading system also plays a fundamentally important role in global food security. For example, it ensures that temporary or protracted food deficits arising from adverse climatic and other conditions can be met from world markets.

Concerns had been expressed about the possible impact of the WTO-AoA on poverty and food security in LDCs and net food-importing countries before the conclusion of the Uruguay Round (Husain 1993), and after the Agreement became effective (FAO 1999; Michalopoulus 1999, 2000). However, it has been noted that the predicted price increases and volatility would depend on the pace of agricultural liberalization in the OECD countries and the specific response to the Agreement of the (developing) countries with comparative advantage in agriculture. Furthermore, changes in world food prices reflect the on-going liberalization of agriculture in developed countries rather than the WTO-AoA per se (Page and Davenport, 1994).

Agricultural trade liberalization, promoted under the AoA, threatens the strong base of farmer-oriented agriculture in favour of industrialized and mechanized agriculture largely carried out and controlled by transnational commodity producers and traders from developed countries. The consequence is often a de facto discrimination against the poorest and most vulnerable sectors of society, contrary to human rights. All agricultural products are subject to liberalization under the AoA. This is a concern especially with regard to staple foods that are vital for food security and which can guarantee the right to food. For example, the main food crop of Bhutan, Bangladesh, India, Nepal and Sri Lanka, is rice. A study on the import pattern of food grains in these countries reveals those most are not self-sufficient and are becoming increasingly dependent on rice imports. Over the period 1995 to 1999 the total import of rice in the South Asian region increased by 132 percent. This increases the risk that South Asia will face worsening food insecurity, and with it the adverse affects on the enjoyment of human rights such as the right to food, to health and to an adequate standard of living.

An examination of India's implementation experience since 1995 reveals that the AOA has, in fact, had little role to play in shaping agricultural policies. More importantly, there is little concrete evidence that agricultural trade liberalization has been detrimental to India's food security. In the AoA, trade and commerce come first—in other words, corporate profits take priority over the health of the planet or people (Ravinder, 2005).

For instance, in domestic support, the product-specific support remains negative for most products and below the deminimis for others. Non-product-specific support also remain below the de minimis limit even if calculations are made without taking into account the exemptions for input subsidies for low-income and resource-poor farmers. This has been true of the 1980s and has continued well into the 1990s. It is only with the international prices crashing to extraordinary low levels that for some products, the product specific support may have turned positive, but this too is unlikely to have exceeded de-minimis levels. India continues to use no export subsidies (excepting for alleged subsidization of wheat exports in 2000-01). As for market access, during the Uruguay Round, India bound its tariffs at levels that were among the highest in the world, at 100 percent for raw commodities, 150 percent for processed agro-commodities and 300 percent for most edible oils (with a notable exception of soya oil at 45 percent).

India has also been able to revise tariffs upwards after renegotiations in respect of products in which these had been bound at low levels in past negotiations (including milk powder, rice, maize etc.). Recent declines in tariff rates imply that the applied rate of customs tariff in India has generally been far below the high rates of ceiling bindings for almost all agricultural products. Still, the existing tariff levels have enough water that offers adequate protection to India. Also, when the QRs were removed in April 2001 a "war room" was set up to track imports of about 300 sensitive commodities most of which were agricultural products. Against this background of implementation experience, it is now time to ask if the AoA has threatened India's food security.

An extensive overview of several crops over the past 3 decades suggests that India is competitive in several major agricultural commodities, and that trade liberalization per se would not necessarily have an adverse impact. Commodities such as rice and wheat, India's major staples, are not only efficient import substitutes but also emerge to be export competitive for several years. Most other commodities belonging to the pulses group or coarse cereals appear to be efficient import substitutes, although not export-competitive. Under the circumstances, there is little threat of a deluge of cheap imports on a regular basis. The only major uncompetitive commodity–even as import-substitutes, seems to be oilseeds and edible oils, which are currently produced at high cost in India. Milk (SMP) too may be of some concern here, although trends in the 1990s are encouraging. Overall, Indian agriculture seems reasonably competitive. In conjunction with the adequate protection offered by tariffs, it is evident that the removal of QRs, in particular, and import liberalization in general has not led to any surge in imports. The only commodity group, which has seen dramatic rise in imports, is edible oils, where India is highly uncompetitive.

At the same time, as indicated in the preamble, the AoA recognized non-trade concerns (NTCs) of countries. These NTCs amongst others, included food security and the need to protect the environment.

There are no measures for food security and rural development purposes that are prohibited by the AoA. For instance, public stockholding and domestic food aid, etc. are all exempt as Green Box measures. Similarly, investment and input subsidies to low-income and resource-poor farmers have also been exempted from any reductions for developing countries.

Thus, so far, there has been no constraint imposed by the AoA on India to meet its food security concerns. Under the circumstance, demanding a "food security box" as India has done or a "development box", as some other developing countries have, is quite unnecessary. In fact, they could be losing propositions, since it would only reinforce demands from highly protected developed countries (in Europe and East Asia) to include their multi-functionality concerns as exempt support (Hoda et al., 2002).

The trade-liberalizing impact of the WTO-AoA, at least in the short run, was expected to lead to higher food prices with diverging effects on net food-importing and exporting countries, as the practical outcome of the OECD countries' protectionist regimes has been to lower world market prices. It would also entail significant redistributive impact in both developed and developing countries with gains and losses to producers and consumers, respectively, in the developing countries (Laird, Peters and Vanzetti, 2004). While higher export prices are good for producers (and exporters), they hurt those countries that depend on subsidized imports (and hurt the urban poor) as they face higher food bills (and prices for basic foods). This could undermine food security. The WTO-AoA is expected to have a positive impact on net food-exporting countries because higher world food prices increase export revenues, even if export volumes were to remain fairly stable, or do not fall more than the proportionate increase in price. Thus, depending on the transmission effect of world prices, producer income and their food security could be boosted.

For the group of net food-importing countries, the level and variability of prices induced by the WTO-AoA raise two interrelated issues: first, how would these influence household food security; and second, how to track this impact with regard to the different sections of the community, in particular the urban and rural poor, and producers versus consumers. This in turn raises one conceptual and practical issue—what are the main income (entitlement) sources of the poor, and how will liberalization impact on these? Considering that labour is the income source for most of the poor, how will liberalization affect real wages? And for those poor who earn a part of their income from the production and sale of agricultural products (as in SSA, for example), what will liberalization do to their profits (Panagariya 2002)?

It is enshrined in the Preamble to the Agreement on Agriculture (AoA) that commitments under the reform programme for trade in agriculture should be made in an equitable way among all Members, having regard to non-trade concerns, including food security. Article 20 of the Agreement, which mandates negotiations for continuation of the reform process, also recognizes that non-trade concerns, such as food security should be taken into account in the negotiations (Ministry of Commerce and Industry).

Three areas of exports which have been heavily promoted under the new trade liberalization regime are aquaculture, floriculture and meat. According to the accepted ideology of free trade the export earnings from exports of farmed shrimp, flowers and meat would finance import of food. Any shortfall of productive capacity from growing food for domestic consumption to producing luxury items for consumption by rich northern consumers would be more than made up. However, it is neither efficient nor sustainable for India to produce shrimps, flowers and meat for export. In each case, more food production capacity is destroyed domestically through diversion of resources and destruction of eco-system than the food that can be purchased on global market through exports. India can buy only one fourth the food it could have grown with export earnings from floriculture.

Food security has therefore declined by seventy five percent, and foreign exchange drain increased by more than a ₹ 100 crore. In the case of meat exports, for every dollar earned, India is destroying fifteen dollars worth of ecological functions performed by farm animals for sustainable agriculture. Cattle in India are the sources of organic fertilizers and renewable energy. In the case of shrimp exports, every rupee of export earnings has generated more than five rupee of export earnings has generated more than five rupees of ecological destruction of water, biodiversity, agriculture and fisheries. Industrial shrimp destroys 200 times more area than the actual size of ponds through Stalinization of ground water, pollution of coastal water, destruction of agriculture and mangroves (Chandra, 2004).

Reasons for Food Insecurity in India

The main reasons of food insecurity in India are as under:

Concentration of Land Ownership: Zamindari abolition was one of the most important steps taken in independent India and the most significant instrument of social justice was the land reform legislations in different states to ensure equitable entitlement to land and to prevent concentration of land ownership. Land reforms such as operation Barga which put land back in the hands of the tiller were also introduced in Bengal. However, during the last sixteen, after WTO requirement, globalization and economic reforms in agriculture have in effect meant an undoing of the earlier reform process guided by values of social justice and equitable distribution of resources. While the positive protections afforded to small farmers and poor consumers and to self-reliance in food for the country have been removed, the reform' package has increased the tendency of centralized control over agriculture.

The main argument used for the industrialization of food and corporatization of agriculture is the low productivity of the small farmer. But in terms of food and nutrition productivity per acre, in terms of efficiency in water use, in terms of creation of livelihoods small farms are more productivity than large ones. Even the World Development Report (WDR) has accepted this fact. Even biologically, small diverse farms have higher productivity than large monoculture farms as long as multiple yields are taken into account. FAO data on total farm output confirms this. In India, a 0-5 acre farm had a productivity of ₹ 735/acre while a 35 acre farm had a productivity of ₹ 346/acre.

For instance, Karnataka has amended the Land Reforms Act of 1961, which undoes the radical reforms that made the tillers the owners of land and prevented non-agriculturalists from becoming absentee landowners. Described as 'predatory capitalism and legalized land grab', these amendments reintroduce land leasing, allow non-agriculturalists and industrialists to own land, and remove land ceiling for aquaculture, horticulture, floriculture and housing industry. The government of Maharashtra has relaxed restrictions on conversion of agricultural lands to non-agricultural land. The agricultural Land Ceiling Act has been amended to permit large land holdings leading to skyrocketing land prices (Vandana, 1996).

Water Privatization and Water Monopolies: Trade liberalisation is also leading to the privatization of water and creation of water monopolies. Water is being reduced to a commodity, owned and traded by water giants—Suez, Vivendi, Bechtel, Thames-RWE. The World Bank policy paper on liberalisation of agriculture recommends the creation of 'markets in tradable water rights'. This institution of tradable water rights is a guarantee for diverting water from small farmers to large corporate super farms. In the logic of the market, tradable rights have a tendency to be sold to the highest bidder and hence lead to water-power linked to concentration of wealth, and to over-exploitation and misuse of water, since those who deplete water resources do not have to suffer the consequences of water scarcity.

Besides, aggravating the already severe ecological crisis in water resources, tradable water rights will destroy the social fabric of rural communities and create discord and disintegration. Tradable water rights are based on the assumption that no ecological or social limits should be placed on water use. Such use without limits leads to abuse. For instance, the new Agriculture Policy of Karnataka talks of a shift from "top down to bottom up" approach. What it implies, however, is that the control over water resources will move upwards from small and marginal farmers to large corporations and agribusiness interests who can buy up the "water equity shares" of "water users associations" and establish monopoly control on water.

The massive US$ 200 billion project of River Linking will also rob rural communities of their riparian water rights. The project, the government claims, is justified on grounds of increased food security through increased irrigation. However, higher water use does not translate into higher food production or nutritional security. Green Revolution crops use 5 to 10 times more water than native varieties. Paddy and Sugarcane use 5 to 10 times more than millets, which provide higher nutrition. Food production could be increased five fold without increasing irrigation by shifting to water prudent but nutrition rich millets (Vandana, 2001). The sale of Ganga water to the French company OndeoDegremont (subsidiary of Suez Lyonnaise des Eaux Water Division—the water giant of the world) for the Sonia Vihar water treatment plant in Delhi exemplifies the way privatization of water is being pursued. 635 million litters a day of water would be made available from the Upper Ganga Canal, one of the oldest canals in Western U.P. While Delhi residents will benefit and the company expects to make ₹ 100 million (10 crore) per annum, mainly based on government guarantees as in the Enron/Dabhol project, farmers of Western U.P. will loose ₹ 2 billion annually, the total "investment" by the company. This project will obviously affect the agricultural output and the food security of the region where the canal had been irrigating for more than one century (Vandana et al., 2002). The farmers are understandably agitated and the people staying in the region have opposed the project, asserting that the "Ganga is not for sale".

Weaker Domestic Marketing Reforms: Most importantly, domestic marketing reforms continue to be the weakest link in Indian agriculture. There is no other explanation for the peculiar paradox that India confronts today: where large sections of the more than one billion Indians suffer from poverty, malnutrition and lack easy access to food while the government holds mammoth food stocks (estimated at about 60 million tones) some of which are rotting in the go downs. The Food Corporation of India, which is responsible for procurement, stocking and supplying the Public Distribution System (PDS), is highly inefficient. Leakages from the PDS are huge. Restrictions on private stockholding (through limits), movement of grains and levies (on rice and sugar) all fragment the Indian market. As a result, grain flow from surplus to deficit areas is hindered and with the inefficacy of the PDS system particularly in areas where it is most needed, it is natural that food security becomes a major cause for concern (Hoda et al., 2002).

Patents on Life and Seed Monopolies: Seeds and biodiversity, which have been the common property of farmers and local communities, are being transformed into private property of a handful of corporations—Monsanto, Syngenta, Duport, Dow, Bayer. These chemical giants now control seeds. India, in fact, is losing its biological and genetic resources, the basic wealth of our country, and the biodiversity based knowledge of our local communities mainly through biopiracy.

The piracy and patenting of our rich biodiversity by the MNCs, institutions and individuals especially from the Western world is inflicting great injury to the natural resources of our land and people. If this is not arrested by appropriate legislation and policy measures, there would be incalculable damage done to the nation and the coming generations (Vandana et al., 2002). India is a signatory of the two international treaties that have an impact on the nation's biodiversity wealth and on peoples' rights to use it and conserve it responsibly. These are the Convention on Biological Diversity (CBD) and the Trade Related Intellectual Property Rights (TRIPS) Agreement under the WTO.

India on behalf of a group of countries including Brazil, Bolivia, Cuba, Dominican Republic, Ecuador, Thailand, Peru and Venezuela has submitted a paper to the TRIPS Council of WTO, on "The Relationship Between the TRIPS agreement and the Convention on Biological Diversity and the Protection of Traditional Knowledge", calling for amendments in TRIPS to harmonize it with the CBD. However, at the domestic level, India has harmonized its Biodiversity laws to be consistent with the unamended TRIPS agreement.

The Government of India has enacted new legislations to implement these international obligations which would far reaching implications for the lives and livelihoods of millions of Indian people. The new corporate-driven intellectual property rights regimes (IPRs), especially the Trade Related Intellectual Property Rights Agreement of WTO is leading to seed monopolies and biopiracy. Seeds have been evolved by nature and farmers over millennia. This collective, cumulate heritage is now either being destroyed by introduction of monocultures of non-renewable seeds or being hijacked by global corporations through patents and biopiracy. When a seed is patented or covered by breeders' rights, farmers can no longer save or exchange seed freely.

Seed saving and seed exchange in defined as a "theft" in intellectual property law. The Indian legislations that have an impact on biodiversity and people's rights are: Patent (Second Amendment) Act, 2002; Protection of Plant Variety Protection and Farmers' Rights Act, 2001; and the Biological Diversity Act, 2002. The country has amended its Patent Act, 1970 for the second time, in May 2002, since TRIPS came into force. The first amendment (undertaken in 1999) was to introduce exclusive marketing rights and mail box arrangement to implement Article 70.8 and 70.9 of TRIPS. There are two amendments in the definition of what is not an invention that has opened the floodgates of patenting of genetically engineered seed. First, in Section 3(i) of the Patent Act, 1997, the word "plants" have been omitted. According to Section 3(i), the following is not an invention: 'Any process for the medical, surgical, creative, prophylactic or other treatment of human beings or any process for a similar treatment of animals or plants or render them free of disease or to increase their economic value or that of their products.'

The omission of "plants" from this section implies that a method or process modification of a plant can now be counted as an invention and can hence be patented. Thus the method of producing Bt cotton by introducing genes of a bacterium Bacillus thurengensis in cotton to produce toxins to kill the bollworm can now be covered by the exclusive rights associated with patents. In other words, Monsanto can now have Bt cotton patents in India. The second amendment has also added a new Section 3(j). This allows production or propagation of genetically engineered plants to be counted as an invention, and hence patentable. Section 3(j) excludes as inventions "plants and animals, including seeds, varieties and species and essentially biological processes for production or propagation of plants and animals".

However, the emergence of new biotechnologies is often used to define production of plants and animals through genetic engineering as not being essentially biological. Without such a clear definition, Section 3(j) allows patents on GMOs patentability and hence opens the floodgate for patenting transgenic plants. The language of Section 3(j) is a verbatim translation of Article 27.3 (b) of TRIPs into India law. Article 27.3(b) of TRIPS states: Parties may exclude from patentability plants and animals other than micro organisms, and essentially biological processes for the production of plants or animals other than non-biological and microbiological processes. However, parties shall provide for the protection of plant varieties either by patents or by an effective sui generis system or by any combination thereof. This provision shall be reviewed four years after the entry into force of the Agreement establishing the WTO.

Technologies of Dependency and Corporate Control: One of the key areas of globalization has been the entry of global corporations in the seed sector. Control over seed is control over the food system. Besides controlling seed through patents and intellectual property rights, corporations like Monsanto and Cargill (now owned by Monsanto) are using technologies of dependency to force farmers into seed dependency. The new seeds are non-renewable—they yield a crop, but the crop is useless for seed because of hybrids based on male sterility, and the impending introduction of "terminator" seeds—seeds which are engineered to be sterile. Corporations are breeding seeds that need chemicals—life herbicide resistant varieties. Even varieties like Bt Cotton, need more pesticides because they are prone to more diseases and pests.

Recent Food Crisis

From 2003 to their peak in mid-2008, the international prices of maize and wheat roughly doubled, while rice prices tripled in a matter of months rather than years (Derek, 2010). The laundry list of popular explanations includes rising oil prices, growing bio fuels demand, evolving Asian diets, declining research and development in agriculture, slowing yield growth, low stocks, macroeconomic imbalances, financial speculation, droughts, and export restrictions.

Furthermore, in the absence of micro-credit and technical support, the richer farmers have proved more adept at exploiting opportunities. The subsidy model has therefore disadvantaged the 75 percent of farms which cover less than two hectares. The majority of these smallholdings are rain-fed, vulnerable to drought and flooding associated with the vagaries of a monsoon climate.

According to the government's State of Environment Report 2009, about 15 percent of agricultural land has been degraded through excessive application of subsidized chemicals. And almost a third of India's groundwater aquifers are now classed as critical or semi-critical.

Role of Indian Government to Prevent Food Insecurity

Indian Government has taken number of steps to sustain food security in India. Some of them are as follows:

1. The government favours direct investment in household food security rather than rural infrastructure. It proposes fundamental reform of the long established Public Distribution System (PDS) which offers 180 million poor families the opportunity to purchase food and cooking essentials at discounted prices.
2. Subsidies for farmers appear likely to remain in place. Indeed, the 2008 budget introduced a loan waiver scheme which wrote off debts totalling US$ 14 billion for tens of millions of farmers. This was a response to the mounting tragedy of 90,000 suicides of farmers since 2001, most of

them believed to be related to crippling debts for farm inputs.

3. Development and government agencies are piloting schemes for more sustainable farming practices. There are promising results from community management of groundwater resources, where neighbourhood farmers recognize a shared interest in recharging aquifers. Micro-irrigation sprinkler technologies are attracting widespread interest as the alternative to wasteful flooding methods.
4. As a step towards food security, which has assumed special relevance in view of recent international developments, the National Food Security Mission aims at increasing cereal and pulses production by 20 million tons over a five year period.

The pressures on India are higher given that it is among the very few countries in which the bound tariffs (i.e. maximum tariffs allowed under the WTO regime) are at levels that are significantly higher than most developing countries. It is, however, important for India to maintain tariffs on products that are critical from the point of view of maintaining food security and livelihoods given that the international prices of many of these commodities have remained sticky at low levels in recent years, a point that was made earlier (Biswajit, 2004).

Solution to Food Insecurity in India

Positive actions on India are urgently needed to prevent an escalation of political insecurity resulting from the crises and to ease the burden on poor people. Particular attention should be given to failed states, which face major food security threats and suffer from inadequate state capacity. New forms of coordination between military and diplomacy actions on the one hand, and developmental and market actions on the other, are required

These are set to grow in number, given that food security is a strategic, national defence issue for India, which must, above all, ensure that its 1.1 billion inhabitants are fed. Aware of this:

1. The Indian government is adjusting customs duties to ensure sufficient domestic supply. The government is also monitoring imports of agricultural goods deemed sensitive in nature (for competing directly with nationally-produced goods), such as dairy, fruit, nuts, coffee, tea, grains, food oils and spices.
2. The government may also decide to limit exports in order to preserve national supply and the stability of domestic prices (this happened in 2006 for legume exports). Wheat exports were also prohibited, in February 2007, to contain a rise in domestic prices.
3. Promote pro-poor agricultural growth. Since small farms are predominant in the India and farm sizes are decreasing further, the productivity of smallholder agriculture is key for promoting agricultural growth. It is crucial to expand smallholder access to finance, risk management strategies, inputs, services, and extension, and increase investment in rural infrastructure.
4. Expand social protection and child nutrition. To protect the basic nutrition of the most vulnerable and improve food security, social protection and nutrition actions are also needed. Protective actions, including conditional cash transfers and employment programs, are necessary to mitigate short-term risks, while preventive actions, including school feeding and early childhood nutrition programs with universal coverage, are needed to avoid long-term negative impacts.
5. Government acquires and subsidies the sale of certain commodities through the Public Distribution System (PDS) that is targeted at low-income families. Over the years PDS has become more targeted, while procurement by government agencies has continued to swell. The result has been a substantial increase in stocks, which greatly exceed the levels considered necessary to ensure food security and the costs associated with maintaining these

stocks. Long term interim policy changes have to be brought about in this regard.

Conclusion

Towards this end, a bold, proactive negotiating stand and aligning with those like the Cairns Group or China would be essential. India should also secure SSGs to protect from import surges, particularly for products where international markets are highly distorted. Equally important are "behind the border reforms" of considerable scale and magnitude. Domestic marketing reforms should be undertaken so that there is one integrated market for food within India and restrictions do not prevent inter-regional flows in a timely and efficient manner. In the context, apart from price reform, a crucial link is institutional reform in both procuring and distribution, which must be undertaken to ensure better household food security. Proper targeting of food subsidies and eventually moving on to a food stamp system should also be pursued. In view of global food insecurity, use of biotechnology and innovations in agriculture can improve yields and provide relief to the farmers, say experts.

Every measure should be taken to safeguard the livelihood security of the farmers, the vast majority of whom are resource-poor operating small and marginal holdings. Hunger has always been an issue that needs attention for humanitarian as well as developmental reasons.

Various Indian public and private sector institutions are conducting extensive agriculture and plant research to increase food security and provide nutritionally-enhanced food to meet the nations' growing food and nutrition.

A reversal of neo-liberal policies in agriculture has become absolutely essential to revive the livelihood systems of rural households in India. However, I would like to argue here that resistance to neo-liberalism can be successful only if the struggle is fundamentally linked to the struggle to resolve the old agrarian question. The strength of the resistance to neo-liberalism in India would continue to depend on the mobilization of poor peasants and agricultural labourers around demands that directly relate to their material conditions of life and work. Allowing for diversities, it remains the case that ending discriminations based on class, caste and gender in India depends critically on weakening the material basis of the landlord and upper caste-hegemony in the villages. Imperialism has not changed this basic reality of the Indian village.

There is a fear of further decline in the growth of food grains production due to problems of sustainability and the ongoing diversification efforts in the high-potential areas like Punjab, Haryana and Uttar Pradesh. Interestingly, Punjab, having just 1.5 percent of the geographical area, contributes about 13 percent to food grains production. However, it is now finding it difficult to sustain the existing level of production owing to problems such as decline in the water table, pest resistance in crops, or deteriorating soil health.

The WTO agreement also affects the food security in different way. Hence, it's now the high time to the Government to come out with a new strategy to secure food in India for non-secured people

There is a lurking fear that trade liberalization and consequently, greater integration of Indian agriculture into world markets through removal of restrictions on exports and imports would lead to a deluge of cheap imp orts threatening food security. This would wipe out the production base, creating unemployment and deepening poverty. Similarly, exports of agricultural produce would reduce domestic availability of cheap food. Also, the price volatility accompanying liberalization would push the poor to the very brink of destitution given their limited capacity to bear risks. This is articulated in statements such as this: "importing agricultural commodities into India means importing unemployment into the country".

There is also an overall feeling that the AoA is an 'unequal treaty' unduly favouring the rich countries. In order to evaluate these concerns, it is first and foremost essential to examine what the AoA entails for India, how India has implemented these commitments and in what ways these impinge on India's food security (Hoda et al., 2002). The AoA also recognizes non-trade concerns, such as food security and the protection of the environment would have to be taken on-board while the Agreement was being implemented in member countries. If so, farsighted donor and government investments in raising agricultural productivity, and policies on behalf of stable food production and prices, might go a long way to preventing food crises in the future.

A new Green Revolution is required to deal with the current food security crisis. Spillane (1999) reported that by 2020 ''cereal production will need to increase by 41 percent, meat by 63 percent and roots and tubers by 40 percent without any significant expansion of agricultural area". New agricultural technologies should contribute to food security through increasing the aggregate supply of food. To this end, policies are required to promote agricultural research which could contribute to food security in developing countries, particularly in relation to orphan crops (Michael, 2010).

References

Adlakha, Anil, (2004), "ORIGIN Round Table on Geographical Indications" Annual WTO Public Symposium, 27th May 2004, Geneva.www.wto.org.

Blakeney, Michael (2010), Recent developments in intellectual property and power in the private sector related to food and agriculture. Elsevier Ltd.

Braun, Joachim von, (2009). Threats to Security Related to Food, Agriculture, and Natural Resources–What to Do?. In conference strategic discussion circle EADS, Berlin, March 26.

Chandra, Ramesh, (2004), Globalization, Liberalization, Privatization and Indian Polity. Delhi: Isha Books.

Dhar, Biswajit and MuraliKallummal, (2004). Trade Liberalisation and Agriculture: Challenges before India. Social Scientist, Vol. 32, No. 7/8 (July-August, 2004), pp. 48-51.

Headey, Derek, (2010), Rethinking the global food crisis: The role of trade shocks. Elsevier Ltd.

Hoda, Anwarul and Ashok Gulati, (2002) Indian Agriculture, Food Security and the WTO-AoA" In: Conference on Economic Reforms and Food Security–The Role of Trade and Technology .ICRIER-ICAR-IFPRI, New Delhi, April 24-25.

Kumar, Ganesh. (2002), Food Security and the WTO Agreement on Agriculture, Agricultural and Mineral Commodities Yearbook, London: Europa Publications.

Lalitha, N. (2004), Diffusion of agricultural biotechnology and intellectual property rights: emerging issues in India, Ecological Economics, pp. 187-198.

Ministry of Commerce and Industry, (2001 January), India and the WTO, A monthly Newsletter, Vol. 3, No. 1, New Delhi.

Murphy, Sophia, (2010), Trade and Food Reserves: What role does the WTO play, IATP.

Paarlberg, Robert L., (2002), "Governance and Food Security in an Age of Globalization", International Food Policy Research Institute. www.ifpri.org.

Ronald, Bind Samuel (2006), Market Access for Agricultural Products, www.scribd.com.

Salih, S. A. (1994), Food Security in East and Southern Africa, Northern Journal of African Studies, 3 (1): 3-28.

Shiva, Vandana, (2004), The Future of food: Countering globalization and recolonisation of Indian agriculture, Elsevier.

Sreenath, Lalitha and M.R. Sreenath, (2006), Impact of Post-TRIPS IP Regime on Indian Agriculture, The Chartered Accountant.

Srinivasan, T.N. and Suresh D. Tendulkar, (2002), Reintegrating India with the World Economy. Washington, DC: Brookings Institution Press.

Stevens, Christopher, Romilly Greenhill, Jane Kennan and Stephen Devereux, (2000), The WTO Agreement on Agriculture and Food Security. Amazon.co.uk.

Timmer, C. Peter, (2009), Reflections on food crises past, Elsevier Ltd.

Timmer, C. Peter, (1986), Getting Prices Right: The Scope and Limits of Agricultural Price Policy, Ithaca: Cornell University Press.

V. Shiva (1997), Biopiracy: The plunder of nature and knowledge. US: Southend Press.

V. Shiva, H.B. Radha and H. Jafri Afsar (2002), Corporate hijack of biodiversity, Navdanya, New Delhi.

V. Shiva, (2001), The violence of green revolution: agriculture, ecology and politics in the south Goa: Other India Press.

V. Shiva, (2003), Will Cancun go the Seattle way? The breakdown of WTO's agriculture negotiations, Cancun Series No. 1, RFSTE/Navdanya.

7

Agricultural Marketing Reforms for Vertical Co-ordination and Integration

Anamika Kaushiva

The development process of the agricultural sector in any economy follows the path of 'commoditisation to commercialisation'. Initially, the agricultural sector of any economy is commodity oriented i.e. supply driven wherein the emphasis is on production of bulk commodities which are sold in spot markets. At this stage, consumers demand undifferentiated commodities at low cost. The purchase or procurement of agriculture produce is based on market-pricing mechanism or price signals. The production system at the commoditisation stage is cost effective. With development and improvement in the standard of living, agriculture transition towards commercialisation begins. The important reasons for this change are as under:

1. Consumer demand changes from undifferentiated commodities to differentiated products with rise in standards of living and diversification of food consumption basket at household level. The food basket in India has undergone a significant change over the last two decades or so. Per capita consumption of different high-value food products between 1983 and 1999 increased by 24 to 39 percent, as against a 16 percent decline in cereal consumption.
2. Rapid economic and income growth, increasing urbanization, changing consumer preferences triggers growth in domestic demand for high-value food products. For the last two decades Indian economy has been growing at an annual rate of over 6 percent, per capita income at 4

percent, and the urban population at 3 percent.

3. Expansion of global market for high-value food commodities results due to globalisation. The share of fruits and vegetables in the world agricultural trade, for example, increased to 19 percent in 2002-03 from 14 percent in 1980-81. In India, high-value food products (fruits, vegetables, dairy products, meat, eggs and fish) accounted for 35 percent of total agricultural exports in 2002-03, as against only 24 percent in 1980-81. The annual growth in exports of high-value food products during this period was 4.4 percent, as compared to 3.5 percent in total agricultural exports.
4. Structural changes in the market towards value addition shift the focus to the final food products. These changes act as an incentive for vertical integration.
5. The agro-processing industries emerge and slowly begin to integrate backward to own the sources of supply to achieve assured supply of raw material reduce transaction costs and minimise losses.
6. The entrepreneurs and firms begin to see new economic opportunities in the farm sector—manufacturing value products and earning higher profit margins in the food processing industry like edible oil, biscuits, alcoholic beverages, and processed foods.

This process of 'commoditisation to commercialisation' cycle requires coordination of links between production, processing and marketing to accommodate manufacture of products based on consumer driven demand. Products with homogeneous product specifications require qualitatively homogeneous supply of agricultural raw materials. This is possible only after an alteration in the existing interface between production and marketing of food products.

Indian Agricultural Market

The development of Indian agriculture till the nineties remained supply driven. The producer was de-linked from the markets, emerging demand pattern and more important from changing consumer preferences. The system did not keep pace with the requirements of the emerging demand patterns and consumption preferences. The evidence of these imperfections is reflected in the existing food grain surplus. No doubt the existence of this food grain surplus implies food security and stabilization of rural income, the need of the hour is generation of larger resource investment in the rural economy. Steps have to taken for improving agricultural productivity, for sustainable use and augmentation of resources and for diversification of the agriculture production system.

The problems of small holdings, seasonality and traditional production and management practices constrain Indian agriculture and force it to remain a dominantly supply driven system. The mismatch between supply and demand in case of agricultural commodities results due to the inability of the farmers to forecast the exact demand, changing nature of consumption pattern and lack of efficiency of commodity markets.

Constraints: These are as under:

1. Predominated by marginal and small farmers with small marketable surplus.
2. Restriction on sale of produce outside regulated market yards.
3. Exploitation by multiple intermediaries—the number of unregulated markets in the country is substantially large. Arhatiyas and brokers, taking advantage of the ignorance, and illiteracy of the farmers, use unfair means. The farmers are required to pay arhat (pledging charge) to the arhatiyas, "tulaii" (weight charge) for weighing the produce, "palledari" to unload the bullock-carts and for doing other miscellaneous types of allied works, "garda" for impurities in the produce, and a number of other undefined and unspecified charges.
4. High cost of transport and marketing in regulated wholesale markets. Only a small number of villages are

joined by railways and pucca roads to wholesale markets. Produce has to be carried on slow moving transport vehicles which cannot be used to carry produce to far-off places and the farmer has to dump his produce in nearby markets even if the price obtained in these markets is considerably low.

5. High post harvest losses and wastage—there is an absence of proper ware housing facilities in the villages. The farmer is compelled to store his products in pits, mud-vessels, "Kutcha" storehouses, etc. These unscientific methods of storing lead to considerable wastage. Approximately 1.5 percent of the produce gets rotten and becomes unfit for human consumption.
6. Lack of standardisation, grading and certification. Different varieties of agricultural produce are not graded properly. The practice usually prevalent is "dara" sales wherein heap of all qualities of produce are sold in one common lot Thus the farmer producing better qualities is not assured of a better price. Hence there is no incentive to use better seeds and produce better varieties.
7. Limited access to information on markets and opportunities—it is often not possible for the farmers to obtain information on exact market prices in different markets. So, they accept whatever price the traders offer to them.
8. Limited bargaining power of producers.
9. Inadequate credit facilities—being poor, farmers try to sell off the produce immediately after the crop is harvested though prices at that time are very low. The safeguard of the farmer from such "forced sales" is to provide him credit so that he can wait for better times and better prices. Since such credit facilities are not available, the farmers are forced to take loans from money lenders, while agreeing to pledge their produce to them at less than market prices.

Keeping in mind the above constraints, policy changes are

required for driving agriculture towards greater market orientation. The best method for imparting market-orientation to Indian agriculture is through dissemination of market information, linkage with agro-processing sector and promotion of competition and transparency of agricultural produce markets. The assessment of demand through better understanding of agricultural markets and the alignment of supply to demand alone can lead to diversification of agriculture production.

Vertical Co-ordination and Vertical Integration

Vertical coordination is a comprehensive term including all means of vertically harmonising exchange between two successive stages in a market channel, e.g., between growers and processors or manufacturers. It is a process of ensuring that each successive stage in the production, processing, and marketing of a product is appropriately managed and interrelated to the next, so that decisions about what to produce and how much, are communicated as efficiently as possible from the consumer to the producer. It synchronises successive stages of production and marketing.

Vertical integration means a system wherein each individual farm loses its identity and becomes a company-owned farm. The company owns or leases the land, buildings and equipment and has its own employees. It is, thus, the ownership of both production and processing. The transaction costs are reduced by internalising production and processing assets. The uncertainty of supply, quality and size is greatly reduced but not totally eliminated due to the high cost of information. Vertical integration is a mechanism that relies upon centralised control to achieve coordination. It helps in achieving higher profits from at least two sources, i.e., efficiency gains of expanded production and partial backward integration may result in a reduction in the dominant firm's acquisition price for externally supplied raw inputs.

Vertical coordination is chosen over vertical integration

because of its flexibility. It allows firms to obtain inputs with specific characteristics without getting into another business (farming) where large investments in specific assets are required. Vertical coordination reduces uncertainty for the farmer and provides a more stable income while allowing him to maintain ownership of his business.

Vertical coordination in the food and agribusiness sector is needed to shift part of the marketing effort toward discovery of consumer preferences rather than manipulation of the same by the retailers. Balancing demand expansion with production increases requires the integration of production with marketing i.e., integrating demand-side research with production-side research. Agricultural expansion in this situation requires newer type of linkages between the participants in the food chain from producer to consumer. The existing linkages in India are conditioned by price signals between various levels and therefore must be replaced by newer linkages based on better information flows and information sharing with regard to product specifications of agricultural raw materials. Such information sharing will lead to qualitatively improved coordination of production and marketing activities. In agriculture four types of vertical coordination between farmers and off-farm businesses exist viz., coordination without any contract (spot market or open market), contract farming, and ownership integration and farmer cooperatives. Amongst these types of vertical coordination, contract farming is becoming an important part of agribusiness and a preferred means of backward integration by the firms needing reliable supply and quality of agricultural raw material.

Production linkages include backward and forward linkages, or, to use an alternative terminology, up-stream and down-stream linkages. Backward production linkages refer to linkages from the farm to the part of the non-farm sector that provides inputs for agricultural production, for example agrochemicals. Forward production linkages refer to the part of the non-farm sector that uses agricultural output as an input.

The distribution and processing of agricultural outputs are fundamental components of forward production linkages.

Expenditure linkages refer to the fact that households deriving income from one type of activity, farm or non-farm, are likely to spend that income on products of other activities. Farmers buy non-farm products with income generated from agriculture. Local entrepreneurs and wage earners use income from the sale of non-farm products to buy food and other agricultural outputs. Expenditure linkages can be divided into consumption and investment linkages. Consumption linkages refer to expenditures related to household consumption; investment linkages refer to expenditure used to finance farm or non-farm activities. Investment linkages can be particularly important within households. Returns on farm activities may be invested to initiate or expand non-farm activities and vice versa.

Three important core processes, which seem to be critical in establishing effective agriculture-market linkages, are:

1. Building effective backward linkages.
2. Conduct and performance of markets and marketing institutions.
3. Demand generation through value addition.

In establishing backward linkages, contract farming, promotion of alternative vertical coordination mechanisms like multi-agency strategic alliances, cooperatives and open market reforms to promote competition and price discovery play an important role. In addition, the backward linkages can also be strengthened through institutional interventions in the form of SHGs at the grass-root level to improve small holders' economies of scale and establishment of farmer markets to provide direct market access to farmers and agricultural futures to strengthen price discovery mechanisms. Secondly, the conduct of markets and marketing institutions can be improved through regulation, competitive setting and favourable policy environment leading. The third critical process in building effective agriculture-market linkage is of 'demand generation through value addition' either through marketing and/or agricultural raw materials. The value addition through marketing can involve practices like commodity promotion programmes, branding commodities, primary processing and manufacturing highly differentiated products.

Evolution of Backward and Forward Linkages in India

The process of evolution of linkage between the producers and agro-industry in India began with the formation of Anand Pattern Cooperatives (AFC) in early 1950s. The process picked up again after a long gap of nearly four decades through public interventions and private sector initiatives in early 1990s, soon after liberalization of the Indian economy.

Anand Pattern Co-operatives (APC): The APC was the first organizational approach of its kind in agriculture commodity sector that attempted development of dairy sector in an integrated manner. The APC went on to prove the extent to which modern dairy technology and institutions can be utilized to minimize the exploitation of small milk producers in free but imperfect markets; enhance their share in consumer rupee and at the same time ensure the all round development of a viable and efficient dairy economy. The structure of APC model is such that even though base production is on a very small scale, the economies of scale for various operations are made directly accessible to individual producers, while vertical integration on the basis of cooperative ownership ensures that the value-added to primary milk is passed on to the primary producers, remaining within the agricultural sector instead of leaking out.

Small Farmers Agri-business Consortiums (SFACs): The other public intervention in promoting vertical coordination was made during the budget proposal of 1992 in the name of Small Farmers' Agri-business Consortium (SFAC), which became operational by 1994-95. The SFAC was registered as public-private joint venture society and has also been declared as a financial institution under Reserve

Bank of India Act, 1934. The basic objective of SFAC is to catalyse agro-industrial growth and pave the way for establishment of integrated producers' organisations with forward and backward linkages. Its main objective is to undertake or assist in undertaking programs for employment generation, growth and diversification of agriculture and agro-based industries, to identify and promote post-harvest processing/manufactures units, to promote organization of marketing chain both for domestic and export marketing and thereby pave the way for establishment of integrated producers' organizations with forward and backward linkages Some of the programmes/schemes being implemented by SFAC society are:

1. Providing schematic pattern of assistance out of GOI grants-in-aid for promotion of value addition in the hands of farmers, through setting up part-processing, semi-processing and full-processing facilities, through the setting up of agri-business ventures all over the country.
2. Functioning as a venture capital fund, and providing assistance to agri-business projects involving value addition in the hands of the farmers.
3. Scheme of Technology Mission for Integrated Development of horticulture in the North Eastern Region of India for development of backward and forward linkages in a holistic manner.
4. Scheme for setting up of a network of agri-clinics and agri-business centres, to train agricultural graduates for servicing the needs of the farmers.

Currently, the SFAC is engaged in diverse activities in fifteen states. SFAC has managed to rope in Godrej Foods and NAFED for manufacturing and marketing of exotic juices—passion fruit seabuckthorn, a wonder berry (energy enhancing drink).

Private Sector Initiatives: The private sector initiatives started in an organised way with the entry of Pepsi Foods Pvt. Ltd. into contract farming of tomato in Punjab in 1989. The

Pepsi model is essentially based on the principle that location-specific R&D leads to profit enhancement over the whole range of crops. R&D to processing and distribution, are fully integrated in the model.

Tata Rallis: The Tata Rallis, in the process of marketing the key farm inputs, including agri-chemicals, pesticides, seeds, fertiliser's, etc., have succeeded in leveraging their strength to the benefit of farmers and other partners. These partners include processors interested in raw material procurement for processing and financial service institutional partner to offer credit on inputs to the farmers as well as funding working capital requirements. Additionally, Tata Rallis are utilising their core strength, i.e. distribution of inputs, to undertake location specific R&D and provision of extension service for the benefit of the farmers.

ITC e-Choupal: In an increasing consumer-oriented business environment, information technology has enhanced and hastened coordination. Information technology has facilitated, if not caused the shifting of marketing effort toward discovery of consumer preferences rather than manipulation of the same by the retailers. Information technology is a means of coordinating activities across levels in order to assure certain product attributes. The use of information technology ensures that the consumer can also evaluate additional characteristics of available products which were previously experienced only indirectly, viz., product quality, nutrition, food safety and in addition to traditional aspects like variety, convenience, price stability, and value etc.

New reforms being introduced in the agricultural sector are making an attempt to promote vertical coordination as shown in the above figure through use of information technology and e-Chaupal is the best example. The e-Choupal model promoted by ITC is specifically designed to resolve the problems that are associated with small and fragmented farm holding, weak infrastructure, supply chain intermediaries and most importantly due to the lack of quality and real time information.

For rural centric growth information technology can make a big impact in creating vertical coordination in Indian food chain. Updated knowledge about weather forecast, crop cultivation practices, post harvest technology, water management through satellite tracking, commercial information, market information for grains, fruits and vegetables, processed food, low cost technology, government schemes and policies on agriculture and agribusiness can be made easily accessible to rural masses through information technology development at rural places.

ITC has set up small 'Internet Kiosks' at the village level to provide farmers real time market and pricing related information and highlighting arbitrage opportunity in sales between various Mandis. It is also involved in providing information related to prices, availability of inputs, weather data and other information related to the agricultural sector. These kiosks are manned by local level lead farmers called "Sanchalaks" who transmit back to the company, information that enables ITC to respond effectively to procurement challenges. ITC is also involved in providing online extension services.

AGMARKNET: At the macro level the policy makers realized that there was a need to make agriculture more responsive to demand, i.e., achieving greater market orientation. This orientation could be achieved only by providing information, technological and marketing support to farmers. The Agriculture Market Information Network (AGMARKNET) was launched keeping this objective in mind. At operational level, the generic framework of AGMARKNET identifies the process of establishing effective backward linkages. The sub-processes include strengthening open marketing system for agricultural commodities and promoting vertical coordination between agriculture and industry in cases where the end-use markets have very specific raw material/product requirements. With regard to open markets, the government's objective is to remove all hurdles in free movement of commodities apart from ensuring competition and technical improvements in trading.

A Nationwide network for speedy collection and dissemination of market information and data was launched in the ninth plan with 210 nodes and expanded to more than 2800 nodes in X plan. The NIC states/districts trained 5000 market personnel to operate the nodes. The project covers 300 commodities, 2000 varieties and 10 languages. The information offered on AGMAKNET Portal includes, prices and arrivals (maximum and minimum, MSP, weekly/monthly prices), arrival trends, future prices from national commodity exchanges, grades and standards, rules of AGMARK, CODEX, commodity profiles of goods like rice, wheat, gram, soybean market profiles i.e. contact details, rail/road connectivity information, infrastructural facilities available, market charges etc.

Reform Measures Proposed

Agriculture sector needs well functioning markets with dynamism and efficiency. For this large investments are required for the development of post harvest and cold chain infrastructure nearer to the farmers' field. Projection of production and marketable surplus of various farm products was assessed by a Task Force set up by the Ministry of Agriculture which estimated that an investment of ₹ 12,230 crore in Tenth Plan would be necessary for infrastructure development for agricultural marketing. Alongside, enabling policies need to be put in place to encourage procurement of agricultural commodities directly from farmers' field and to establish effective linkage between the farm production and the retail chain and food processing industries. Towards this end, the Inter-Ministerial Task Force on Agricultural Marketing Reforms constituted by this Ministry in its report made the following important recommendations:

1. Promoting competitive agricultural markets in private and

cooperative sectors, direct marketing and contract farming programmes by amending the State Agricultural Produce Marketing Regulation Acts and providing central assistance for the development of marketing infrastructure subject to such deregulation and reforms.

2. Dismantling controls and regulations under the Essential Commodities Act to remove all restrictions on production, supply, storage and movement of, and trade and commerce in respect of all agricultural commodities.
3. Increasing flow of institutional credit to farmers for marketing of crops (pledge financing) to enhance their holding capacity to obtain remunerative price for their produce.
4. Expand availability of warehousing services in rural areas by introducing negotiable warehousing receipt system for agricultural commodities.
5. Allowing futures trading in all agricultural commodities to improve price risk management and facilitate price discovery by amending the Forward Contracts (Regulation) Act, 1952.

The recommendations contained in these Reports were discussed with the State Governments at a National Conference on September 27, 2002 and later by a Standing committee of State Ministers on January 29, 2003. In view of liberalization of trade and emergence of global markets, it was necessary to promote development of a competitive marketing infrastructure in the country. Along with these measures steps are also needed to put in place adequate safeguards to avoid any exploitation of farmers by the private trade and industries through model legislation on agricultural marketing. Accordingly following measures have been initiated:

1. Model APMC Act.
2. Alternative marketing systems–private/cooperative markets, modern terminal markets, contract farming etc initiated.
3. Dismantling of controls and regulations under EC Act.

4. Law for implementing Negotiable Warehouse Receipts System passed by Parliament.
5. Reform Linked Assistance to encourage private investment for development of marketing infrastructure, integrated supply chain and grading facilities.
6. Storage facilities in rural areas.
7. Development of cold chain, refrigerated transportation, perishable cargo centres.
8. E-trading through Electronic Spot Exchange.
9. AGMARKNET–Market information system.
10. Improvement in Marketing and distribution through measures like ITC E-chaupal, Mahindra Shubh Labh, Haryali Kisan Bazar.
11. Commodity Exchanges like, NCDEX, MCX, National Electronic Spot Exchange Ltd.

Sustained economic and income growth, fast growing urban population and increasing integration of global agri-food markets are fuelling rapid growth in demand for high-value food commodities in India. This is an opportunity for the farmers especially smallholder farmers to augment their income and utilize surplus family labour in production of high-value labour-intensive food commodities. Improving smallholders' access to markets requires close linkages between farmers, processors, traders, and retailers to coordinate supply and demand. Institutions such as cooperatives, producers' associations, and contract farming are important means of linking producers with markets, as well as a source of credit, inputs, technology, information and services. But, there is an apprehension that smallholders may be excluded from the institution-driven value chains. There is also a fear that agribusiness firms may exploit smallholders by extracting monopsonistic rent in the output market and manipulating terms and conditions of the contract. If the policies are implemented and regulated these fears would be short lived and new opportunities will emerge for the farm sector.

References

Birthal P.S., P.K. Joshi, (2006) Small Farmers Access to Markets for High Value Agricultural Commodities in India.

Chauhan U.K.S., Department of Agriculture and Cooperatives, MoA, GOI: Market Reforms in India–Making Markets Work for Farmers.

Mittal. S. (2006), Structural shift in demand for food: projections to 2020. Working Paper No. 184, Indian Council for Research on International Economic Relations, New Delhi, India.

Parthasarathy Rao, P., P.S. Birthal and P.K. Joshi, (2006) Diversification towards high-value agriculture: Role of Urbanization and Infrastructure, Economic and Political Weekly, June 30.

Vaswani Prof. L.K, Dr. V Venkateshvaran, Mr. R Upadhyay, Mr. J. Talati, (2003), Agriculture–market Linkages: Evaluating and Evolving a conceptual Framework in Indian Context, NABARD.

8

Marketing of Mutual Funds in Rural Areas

Ranjit Singh and Anurag Singh

Introduction

A mutual fund is a trust that pools the savings of a number of investors who share a common financial goal. The money thus collected is then invested in capital market instruments such as shares, debentures and other securities. The income earned through these investments and the capital appreciations realized are shared by its unit holders in proportion to the number of units owned by them.

Thus, a mutual fund is the most suitable investment for the common man as it offers an opportunity to invest in a diversified, professionally managed basket of securities at a relatively low cost.

Like most developed and developing countries the mutual fund cult has been catching on in India. The most important characteristic of a mutual fund is that the contributors and the beneficiaries of the funds are the same class of people, namely the investors. A mutual fund's business is to invest the funds thus collected, according to the wishes of the investors who created the pool. In many markets these wishes are articulated as "investment mandates." Usually, the investors appoint professional investment managers, to manage their funds.

The same objective is achieved when professional investment managers create a "product," and offer it for investment to the investor. This product represents a share in a pool, and pre- stated investment objectives. For example, a mutual fund which sells a "money market mutual fund," is actually seeking investors willing to invest in a pool that would invest predominantly in money market instruments.

For the individual investor, mutual funds provide the benefit of having someone else manage their investments and diversify their money over many different securities that may not be available or affordable to them otherwise. Today, minimum investment requirements on many funds are low enough that even the smallest investor can get started in the mutual funds.

Growth of Mutual Fund Industry in India

Mutual funds have been there in India for around a long period of time to be precise for 36 years. But it was the year 1999 that saw immense future potential and developments in this sector. This year signalled the year of resurgence of mutual funds and the regaining of investor confidence in these Mutual Funds. This time around all the participants are involved in the revival of the funds that is the AMC's, the unit holders, the other related parties. However, the sole factor that gave life to the revival of the funds was the Indian Union Budget of 1999 (Finance Act, 1999).

The budget brought about a large number of changes in one stroke. It provided centre stage to the mutual funds, made them more attractive and provides acceptability among the investors. The Union Budget exempted mutual fund dividend given out by equity-oriented schemes from tax, both at the hands of the investor as well as the mutual fund. As a result there was the aggressive expansion of the foreign owned mutual fund companies along with the companies floated by the nationalized banks and smaller private sector players.

After such a big boost give to the mutual fund industry, now the mutual fund industry is growing in a phenomenal way. There were several numbers of national as well as international players entered into the Indian market and trying to penetrate the Indian market. Now no longer were the mutual funds interested in selling the concept of mutual funds rather they wanted to talk business which would mean to increase asset base, and to get asset base and investor base they had to be fully armed with a whole lot of schemes for every investor. So, the new fund offers were inevitable.

The quest to attract investors extended beyond just new schemes. This includes opening up the offices at the small towns, designing the schemes for the poor people with small amount of money to be invested etc. One can say that the industry is moving from infancy to adolescence, the industry is maturing and the investors and funds are frankly and openly discussing difficulties opportunities and compulsions.

Marketing of Mutual Funds in Rural India

With the increasing competition for penetrating the market of mutual funds every day mutual funds are coming up with new strategies to tap the market. It includes providing better services to designing new products. For example, Reliance Mutual Fund has brought a scheme for the small investors to invest as low as ₹ 50 per month in mutual funds. This scheme has received considerable response from the investor's community. It has given a chance especially to the rural investor also to invest in the rural market. Some of the banks in the rural areas are selling the mutual funds.

It is believed that the urban market is almost saturated and only mantra for the survival is to expand its services in the rural India. This market is still untapped. But in order to spread its wings in the rural India, the mutual fund companies must consider some of the peculiarities of the rural India. Then only they will be successful in marketing their services in the rural areas.

The Indian rural market with its vast size and demand base offers a huge opportunity that mutual funds cannot afford to ignore. With 128 million households, the rural population is nearly three times the urban. As a result of the growing affluence, fuelled by good monsoons and the increase in agricultural output to 200 million tons in year 2000 from 176 million tons in year 1991, rural India has a large consuming class with 41 percent of India's middle-class and 58 percent of the total disposable income.

The importance of the rural market for some FMCG and durable marketers is underlined by the fact that the rural market accounts for close to 70 percent of toilet-soap users and 38 percent of all two-wheeler purchased. The rural market also accounts for half the total market for TV sets, fans, pressure cookers, bicycles, washing soap, blades, tea, salt and toothpowder. The rural market for FMCG products is growing much faster than the urban counterpart.

It is evident from the above facts that there is enormous potential to the mutual funds also to penetrate into the rural market.

The rural market may be appealing but it is not without its problems. These are low per capita disposable incomes that is half the urban disposable income; large number of daily wage earners, acute dependence on the vagaries of the monsoon; seasonal consumption linked to harvests and festivals and special occasions; poor roads; power problems; and inaccessibility to conventional advertising media.

It means that in order to offer its services in the rural areas mutual funds have to change their strategies. They cannot follow the same strategies which are being followed in the urban areas.

4 A's of Marketing

Traditionally, any companies trying to market its product have to adhere to the four elements of marketing mix that are known as 4Ps of marketing. These are product, price, promotion and place. But in order to survive in the rural market the mutual funds have to focus on 4A's of marketing instead of 4P's of marketing. These are affordability, availability, awareness and acceptability of the products (Prahalad, 2005).

Affordability of Mutual Funds by Rural People: Here affordability means that product and services should be in the reach of rural customers. It means product should be in the buying capacity of rural customer. If want to be successful in rural or suburban market the financial companies will have to ensure affordable products or services. The income level of sub urban and rural house hold is limited. They are either dependent on salary, wages or agriculture. BOP customers have low disposable incomes, and products need to match the cash-flows of customers who frequently receive their income on a daily rather than weekly or monthly basis (Srivastava, S., 2003). Two-thirds of Indian villagers are in the bottom income band making them acutely sensitive to price, and more than two-thirds of their income is typically spent on food.

It is estimated that there are about 180 million households in India, of which only 10 million have invested in mutual funds. In urban areas, 13.7 percent of households have mutual funds while in rural or sub urban areas it is just 3.8 percent. It indicates that there is a lot of scope for the growth of mutual fund companies in India provided there are funds to satisfy everybody's requirement sharp improvement in service standards and disclosure (Rama Murthy, B. M. and Reddy, S., 2005). Mutual funds are affordable in the way as it accommodate rural investors who don't have a lot of money to invest by setting relatively low amount investment for initial purchases, subsequent monthly purchases or both (Debra, 2005). Their simplicity, accessibility and affordability make them popular with both novice and seasoned investors. Investors can invest as little as ₹ 500 (David M., 2009).

Affordability is a key consideration for most mutual fund investors. The rural investors of mutual fund do not have huge estate to invest but yes they are the small amount contributor to the fund. Some time they come as one time investor and some time on monthly basis. Being able to pay into an investment on a monthly basis, provides the mutual fund greater access to a larger investment community (Learner D., 2007).

Availability of Mutual Funds in Rural Areas: One of the biggest challenges of serving sub urban and rural markets is to ensure availability of products and services. Once product reaches the market there will not be a problem of selling due to lesser availability of brands in the market. The task to simply getting products to people is a major hurdle of sub urban and rural market. Consider the challenge facing companies wishing to target low-income consumers in India's, which are spread over 3.2 million square kilometres. In many parts of the country roads are little more than rutted dirt tracks, and in the monsoon season these can be literally washed away. In hilly area, roads to isolated villages cut across snow-covered mountain passes that can be closed for weeks at a time. The time to cover even small distances under such conditions can be long.

Sustainable growth of citizens depends on the availability of the financial product (Okpala, 1994). The central issues of focus are sustainable availability, affordability and accessibility of financial products like housing finance and mutual fund to sub urban and rural households (Okpala, 1994). There is a need to formulate strategies for the dispersion of mutual funds to semi-urban and rural markets (Thingalaya, 2005). One day urban market will reach the saturation point throughout the world from investment angle and further commoditization will not be possible than investment companies will think to shift their attention to the interest of rural citizens of the country (Rosenzweig, and Binswanger, 1993). Deutsche Mutual Fund plans to turn its attention to companies focused on rural India, courtesy an equity fund titled Deutsche Green India Fund mainly concentrating the rural citizens (Team, 2006). Sustainable growth of any developing country depends on the availability of the financial product as it was stated by Udry (1994) while doing the empirical study in northern Nigeria.

Awareness about Mutual Funds in Rural Areas: Business of any product or services is solely dependent on awareness. A survey done by CAMS (Computer and management services) through IMRB (Indian Market Research Bureau) in a selected location has revealed a startling fact that there is less than 50 percent awareness of funds and less than 50 percent awareness of regulations and returns in the country (Business Line, 2007). Therefore, this is the first requirement of any business to make their customer aware. The awareness programs should be conducted at the junction (Chaupal) where the villagers generally use to meet. The awareness message should contain unique message with concern for them and their places.

Awareness programs should be done in local language so that an illiterate or a layman can understand (Patawari and Jain, 2008). Source of information like banks, agents and news paper are more the part of problem then a solution (Rathore, 2008). Therefore, to be a part of solution awareness information of mutual fund should be loaded on TV, radio, outdoor and face to face awareness program. (Merton, 1987; Lee, 1992; Barber and Odean, 2003) argued that advertising has the ability to increase investors' awareness of a fund or fund family, which would be expected to affect mutual fund flows. As mutual funds creates awareness among urban and rural middle class people about the benefits of investment in capital market, through profitable and safe avenues, mutual fund could be able to make up a large amount of the surplus funds available with these people (Tripathy N., 1996).

The mutual fund industry is planning to launch a series of investor awareness programs in the rural and sub urban part of the country, in an attempt to improve retail penetration. A decision to this effect was taken at the board meeting of the Association of Mutual Funds in India (AMFI). Fund houses apparently have agreed to conduct at least 8-10 investor awareness programs every month. The cost of such programs will be borne by the fund itself. India's largest MF Reliance Mutual Fund, conducts around 75-100 awareness programs every month but they call it a work site presentation where they give basic knowledge of the mutual funds (Madia, 2010).

Acceptability of Mutual Fund in Rural Areas: Bending to fit in is of vital importance to gain acceptability in the rural market. Service providers must conduct a basic ground level research to zero down on the niche areas that would suit the rural market. LG Electronics' Sampoorna, a customized TV made exclusively for the rural market was a great hit, so is Coca-Cola's introduction of chota coke and low-cost-ice-boxes instead of refrigerators, as electricity is not a premium in the rural areas. The centre of idea is to offer products and services that are adapted to the unique needs of both customers and distributors. Similar kinds of initiatives are required to be taken to make the mutual funds acceptable in the rural areas.

Suggestions

From the above discussion the following points can be put forward for penetrating the mutual funds in rural India:

1. As the rural people's main source of income is agriculture, so the mutual fund should be designed in such a way that the people should be allowed to invest during the harvesting season instead of monthly basis.
2. Making investment on the daily basis can be thought of as the people have very low disposable income and moreover, agriculture labourers are the daily wage earners therefore, if they are allowed to make deposit on a daily basis, it will be more affordable to them.
3. One of the biggest challenges of serving rural markets is to ensure availability of products and services on sustainable basis. Mutual funds can be made available in rural India through the effective arrangement with the post offices. The post offices have huge rural network and it can be leveraged for penetrating the mutual funds in rural areas.
4. For the making mutual funds available in rural areas, arrangement can be made in collaboration with the Non-governmental Organisations [NGOs].
5. For increasing the awareness about the mutual funds in

rural areas, the awareness programmes should be conducted in the local language and the use of radio and TV should be considered.

6. The local Gaon Panchayat should also be taken into confidence for conducting awareness programme.
7. The fund offered in the rural areas should be designed in such a way that there should be very low volatility. As the rural people have very small investible amount, any negative fluctuation in their fund value may render the product unacceptable for them. Therefore, the product should be designed in such a way that there is lesser exposure to the equity and more of the government securities and bonds.

Conclusion

It can be concluded from the above review that mutual funds are taking suitable steps to penetrate the rural markets of India. To expand its services in the rural market, it is the need of the hour to design suitable products keeping in view the peculiarities of the rural market. The innovation should also be in the delivery mechanism as well as in the product design so that the designed product can reach to the rural consumers in an effective and efficient way.

References

Barber, Brad, and Terrence Odean, (2003), All that glitters: The effect of attention and news on the buying behaviour of individual and institutional investors, University of California-Davis and University of California-Berkeley working paper.

Business Line, (2007), 'Awareness on mutual fund investments weak' retrieved on 1/5/2010 from http://www.thehindubusinessline.com/2007/08/14/stories/2007081452481500.htm.

Carhart, Mark M., "On Persistence in Mutual Fund Performance," Journal of Finance, Volume 52 (March).

David M, (2009), Mutual fund, retrieved on 2/5/10 from http://www.farmers.com/mutual_funds _insurance.html.

Debra P, (2005), Mutual fundamentals, retrieved on 2/5/2010 from http://www.ag.ndsu.edu/pubs /yf/fammgmt/fe606w.htm.

Kahn, Ronald N., and Andrew Rudd, (1995) "Does Historical Performance Predict Future Performance?" Financial Analysts Journal, Volume 51 (November-December 1995), 43-52.

Kamakodi N., (2008), Looking beyond technology: a study of e-banking channel acceptance by Indian customers, International Journal Electronic Banking, Vol. 1, No. 1, pp. 73- 94.

Kinder, Peter D., and Amy L. Domini, (1997), "Social Screening: Paradigms Old and New." Journal of Investing, Vol. 6, No. 4 (Winter):12-19.

Learner D, (2007), Mutual fund functions retrieved on 1/5/2010 from http://www.ehow.com/list_5886369_mutual-fund-functions.html

Lee, Charles M.C. (1992), Earnings news and small traders, Journal of Accounting and Economics, 15, 265-302.

Madia C, (2010): Mutual funds sets sights on rural, semi-urban markets retrieved on 30/4/2010 from http://www.financialexpress.com/news/mutualfundssetssightsonrural-semiurbanmarkets/600 994.

Mazumdar, N A, (1999), reviving rural credit, *Economic and Political Weekly*, Vol. 34, No. 25, pp. 1577-1579.

Merton, Robert C., (1987), A simple model of capital market equilibrium with incomplete information, Journal of Finance, 42, 483-510.

Okpala D C, (1994), Financing Housing in Developing Countries: A Review of the Pitfalls and Potentials in the Development of Formal Housing Finance Systems, vol 31, No 9, pp 1571 - 1586

Patawari V and Jain A (2008), Mutual Funds for Rural India, retrieved on 1/5/2010 from http://www.managementcanvas.iimindore.in/icanvas/index.php?option=com_content&view=article&id=93:mutual-funds-for-rural-india&catid=35:finance-and-banking&Itemid=54.

Prahalad, C. K. (2005), The Fortune at the Bottom of the Pyramid: Eradicating Poverty Through Profits, Wharton School Publishing .

Rama Murthy B M and Reddy S, (2005), Recent trends in mutual fund industry, SCMS journal of Indian Management, Vol. 2, No. 3, pp 27-32.

Rathore V, (2008), Low awareness of mutual funds snags AMCs' bid to expand base, retrieved on 1/5/2010 from http://www.livemint.com/2008/08/04231928/Low-awareness-of-mutual-funds.html.

Rosenzweig, M. R. and Binswanger H. P., (1993), "Wealth, Weather Risk and the Composition and Profitability of Agricultural Investments" The Economic Journal January (103) 56-78.

Srivastava, S. (2003): "What is the True Level of FDI Flows to India?", Economic and Political Weekly, Volume 38, No. 7, pp. 608-611.

Team E, (2006), Mutual Funds enter rural India, retrieved on 2/5/2010 from http://www.agricultureinformation.com/mag/?p=1813.

Thingalaya, (2005), Need to educate rural population on mutual funds stressed, retrieved on 2/5/2010 from http://www.blonnet.com/2005/06/15/stories/2005061502771700.htm.

Tripathy N, (1996), Mutual Fund in India: A Financial Service in Capital Market, Finance India, Vol. X, No. 1, pp. 85-91.

Udry, C. (1994). "Risk and Insurance in a Rural Credit Market: An Empirical Investigation in Northern Nigeria." Review of Economic Studies 61: 495-526.

Wise, (2009), Wise mutual fund process, retrieved on 1/5/2010 from https://www.wiseequities.com/pdffiles/selectionprocess.pdf.

9

Agriculture Finance in India

A.N. Tamragundi and S.G. Hundekar

Introduction

Agriculture is the backbone of Indian economy. Agriculture encompasses a wide variety of specialties and techniques including ways and means to expand the land suitable for plant raising and other farm activities.

For stimulating the tempo of agriculture production an adequate and timely credit is most essential. Modern agriculture is costly affair and farmers have to rely on outside finance to adopt better techniques of production. There exists strong and positive relationship between agriculture growth and availability of credit. The availability of agriculture credit is in the forms of short-term credit, medium-term credit and long-term credit. The adequate and timely credit to the farmers is a vital and indispensable for rehabilitation and progress of agriculturists.

Presently, India ranks second in the world in farm output. Agriculture is the main source of livelihood of the people of the country. Agriculture is the largest economic sector and plays a vital role in the socio-economic development of India.

The farmers cannot fulfil their credit needs from their savings only. It is because their income from farm operation is sufficient to provide minimum necessities of the life. Agriculture credit is a nucleus of the system of farm operation.

Therefore here an attempt is made to understand the concept of agriculture finance, features, need for agriculture finance, types, and sources of agriculture finance, RBI guidelines and problems of agriculture finance.

India is the largest producer in the world of milk, cashew

nut, coconuts, tea, turmeric, ginger and black pepper. India is also famous for production of wheat, rice, sugar, groundnut, inland fish, tobacco and fruit production.

Importance of agriculture is evident from the following points of information:

1. It is a source of food supply and fodder for animals.
2. It supplies various kinds of raw materials to industries.
3. It earns valuable export foreign exchange through export of agriculture products.
4. It constitutes predominate share in National Income.
5. It improves the rural welfare.
6. It gives employment to a large number of people.
7. It creates demand for industrial products and constitutes expansion of secondary and tertiary sectors.

Large numbers of people depend upon rural employment for a living. Current agriculture practices are neither economically nor environmentally sustainable and India's yield for agriculture commodities are low. The factors responsible for low productivity of agriculture are as follows:

1. Agriculture practices are controlled by customs and tradition.
2. Old and obsolete techniques of production.
3. Lack of improved seeds, fertilizer, pesticides.
4. Poorly maintained irrigation facilities.
5. Poor infrastructure, marketing facilities are inadequate
6. Fragmentation of land holdings.
7. Increasing cost of agriculture because of over regulation, price risks and uncertainty.
8. Government intervention in labour, land and credit markets.
9. Ignorance and illiteracy of agriculturalists.

Among the above factors one of the severe problems faced by agriculturists is "lack of adequate credit facilities".

Finance has been recognized as the life blood of all economic activities. For stimulating the tempo of agriculture production, an adequate and timely credit is most essential.

Modern agriculture is costly affair. Effective arrangements are needed to provide credit facilities, so that agriculturists may adopt better techniques of production.

Problems of Agriculture Finance

The adequate and timely availability of finance will help the farmers to produce the crop at the right time and market the same without any delay. Farmers can market necessary equipments, seeds, fertilizers etc. to get good crop. Thus financing acts as a nuclear of the system of farm operation.

But there are certain problems associated with agriculture finance. They are mentioned as below:

1. Limited coverage of agriculture credit.
2. Complicated procedures are to be made to avail loans. Majority of the farmers are illiterate and are unable to furnish required information to avail credit facilities.
3. Wastage of time and manpower: All financial institutions situated in cities. Farmers have to visit the bank office for a number of times to fulfil many formalities to sanctioning of loans. This leads to wastage of time.
4. Lack of co-ordination: In respect of credit planning, the lack of co-operation exists between co- operatives and commercial banks. So paucity of funds has been greatly responsible for low production of agriculture, thus poverty of cultivators.
5. Mis-utilisation of loans: The gap between disbursement and requirement in the farm sector should be mis-utilised by farmers for unproductive purposes in rural areas of the country.
6. Inefficient administration: Administrative person keen for their personal benefits and do not work for the betterment of farming community.
7. Regional imbalances: The states of Gujarat, Andhra Pradesh, Punjab, Tamil Nadu, and Maharashtra avail 52 percent of total agriculture credit and get rapid growth in crop productivity. Other states lack the credit facilities

leads to low productivity.

Thus, these are the various problems faced by agriculture financing.

Features of Agriculture Finance

1. **Riskiness in Agriculture:** Riskiness may be due to uncertainties (drought, floods etc.) lack of proper marketing and storage facilities, non availability of pesticides etc. So agriculture becomes a costly affair.
2. **Difficulties of Co-operation in Agriculture:** Farmers are mostly individualistic and are suspicious of co-operating with each other for a common purpose. This creates difficulties to farmers in getting credit.
3. **Credit for Consumption Purpose:** Farmers may spend agricultural loan on litigation, social and religions functions. i.e., finance is used for consumption and other non productive purposes.
4. **Small Size of Farms:** More over in the small farms, there is no control over the yield and quality of produce. The amount of labour employed and the extent of capital employed is very low.
5. **Lack of Proper Securities:** Small farmers neither posses proper securities to pledge against loans nor they have adequate repaying capability. Hence, they are forced to go to the money lenders.
6. **Economic Lags in Agriculture:** During agriculture production process, there exists long-interval between reward and effort. The uncertainty becomes an excuse for credit agencies to refuse credit for farm operation.
7. **Complex of Many Industries:** Agriculture is an industrial complex of varying types of production and marketing. The size of land holdings, forms of land tenure differ from one area to another. These differences create complex relations between farmers and makes agriculture sector financing more difficult.

Need for Agriculture Finance

1. For agriculture purposes i.e., to purchase seeds, purchase of livestock, for payment of rent, wages, irrigation of crops, fodder, hire charges of pumps, repairs of agriculture implement, land improvement, for laying orchard and capital expenditure on agriculture.
2. For family expenditure including, credit for the purchase of utensils, clothing, paying for medical, educational and other family expenses.
3. For non-farm business purposes i.e., repair of production and transport equipment, furniture, construction, repair of building and other capital expenditure.
4. For other purposes, including the repayment of old debts, deposits with co-operative agencies, shares, and unspecified purposes etc.

Types of Agriculture Finance

1. Short-term credit to cover operating expenses.
2. Intermediate credit for investing in farm equipment etc.
3. Long-term credit for the acquisition of farm, real estate, construction financing etc.

Sources of Agriculture Finance

Sources of agriculture credit are non-institutional and institutional:

Non-Institutional Credit: It is available from the following sources:

- **Traders and Commission Agents:** These people advance loans to farmers for productive purposes against their crop without completing legal formalities. It becomes obligatory for farmers to buy inputs and sell output through them. They charge high rates of interest of their lending.
- **Land Lords:** For meeting day to day financial requirements small farmers and tenants depend on land lords.

- **Money Lenders:** Agriculture money lenders combine their money lending job with farming. Professional money lenders job is money lending only. Money lenders provide advance to productive as well as non productive purposes against promissory notes or land, very high rates of interest they charge for their lending. Money lenders are easily approachable at odd hours and they require very low paper work.

Institutional Credit: The evolution of institutional credit to agriculture could be broadly into 4 district phases.

- 1904-1969 (Pre dominance of co-operatives and setting up of RBI).
- 1969-1975 (Nationalization of commercial banks and setting up of RRBs).
- 1975-1990 (Setting up of NABARD).
- 1991 onwards (financial sector reforms).

The providers of institutional loans are as follows:

1. **Government:** The government provides both short term and long term loans. Those loans are generally advanced in times of natural calamities. These loans are popularly known as "taccavi loans". The rate of interest chargeable is very low. It is not the major source of Agricultural finance.
2. **Co-operative Societies:** The Government passed Co-operative Societies Act in 1904. The provision for registration of all types of co-operative societies in the credit and non credit areas was passed in the year 1912. In subsequent years a number of committees were appointed to improve the functioning of co-operatives. The co-operatives promote agriculture credit and development of rural areas.
3. **Commercial Banks:** Commercial banks are the largest source of agriculture credit (48 percent). Nationalization of commercial Banks in 1969 induces the banks to play an active role in agriculture credit.
4. **Regional Rural Banks:** RRBs were set up in those areas

where availability of institutional credit was found to be inadequate but potential for agricultural development was very high. RRBs advance to the small and marginal farmers, landless labourers, village artisans for productive purposes. At present 196 RRBs are functioning in the country lending around 9000 crore to rural people particularly to weaker sections.

Lending to Priority Sector: At the meeting of the National Credit Council held in July 1968, it was emphasized that commercial banks should increase their involvement in the financing of priority sectors, viz. agriculture and small-scale industries. It was later formalized in 1972 relating to advances to priority sectors constituted by Reserve Bank of India.

On the basis of the recommendations made in September 2005 by the Internal Working group, set up in Reserve Bank to examine, review, and recommend changes if any in the existing policy on priority sector lending including the segments constituting the priority sector, target and sub target etc. and the comments/suggestions received there on form banks, financial institutions, public and the Indian Banks Association (IBA) it has been decide.

Categories of priority sector include the following:

1. Agriculture (direct and indirect finance).
2. Small enterprises (direct and indirect finance).
3. Other small business/service enterprises.
4. Micro credit.
5. Education loans.
6. Housing loans.

Targets and Sub-targets

Total agriculture advances 18 percent of Adjusted Net Bank Credit (ANBC) or credit equivalent amount of off-balance sheet exposure whichever is higher.

Of this, indirect lending in excess of 4.5 ANBS or credit equivalent amount of off balance exposure, whichever is higher will not be reckoned for computing performance under

18 percent target. However, all agriculture advances under the categories 'direct' and 'indirect' will be reckoned in computing performance under the overall priority sector target of 40 percent of ANBS or credit equivalent amount of off Balance Sheet Exposure, whichever is higher.

Differential Rates of Interest Scheme

1 percent of total advances outstanding as at the end of the previous year. It should be ensure that not less than 40 percent of the total advances granted under DRI scheme go to SCs/STs. At least 2/3 of DRI advances should be granted rural and semi urban branches.

Direct Finance to Agriculture

Finance to individual farmers [including Self-help Groups (SHGs) or Joint Liability Groups (JLGs), i.e., groups of individual farmers, provided banks maintain disaggregated data on such finance] for Agriculture and Allied Activities.

1. Short-term loans for raising crops, i.e. for crop loans. This will include traditional/non-traditional plantations and horticulture.
2. Advances up to ₹ 10 lakh against pledge/hypothecation of agriculture produces (including warehouse receipts) for a period not exceeding 12 months, irrespective of whether the farmers were given crop loans for raising the produce or not.
3. Short-term loans under tie-up arrangements with sugar mills, agro-processing units and agriculture exporters.
4. Working capital and term loans for financing production and investment requirements for agriculture and allied activities.
5. Loans to small and marginal farmers for purchase of land for agriculture purposes.
6. Loans to distressed farmers for purchase of land for agricultural purposes.
7. Loans granted for pre-harvest and post-harvest activities

such as spraying, weeding, harvesting, grading, sorting, processing and transporting undertaken by households or groups/cooperatives of households.

8. Finance to others up to an aggregate amount of ₹ 20 lakh per borrower for the purposes listed at 1 to 4.

Indirect Finance

Finance for Agriculture and Allied Activities:

1. Loans to entities covered under 1 above in excess of ₹ 20 lakh in aggregate per borrower for agriculture and allied activities.

   In such cases, the entire amount outstanding shall be treated as indirect finance for agriculture.
2. Loans to food and agro-based processing units with investment in plant and machinery up to ₹ 10 crore, undertaken by other than households.
3. Loans to Non-Banking Financial Companies (NBFCs) for on lending to individual farmers.
4. Credit for purchase and distribution of fertilizers, pesticides, seeds, etc.
5. Loans up to ₹ 40 lakh granted for purchase and distribution of inputs for the allied activities such as cattle feed, poultry feed, etc.
6. Finance for setting up of agri-clinics and agri-business centres.
7. Finance for hire-purchase schemes for distribution of agricultural machinery and implements.
8. Loans to farmers through Primary Agricultural Credit Societies (PACS), Farmers' Service Societies (FSS) and Large-sized Adivasi Multi Purpose Societies (LAMPS).
9. Loans to cooperative societies of farmers for disposing of the produce of members.
10. Financing the farmers indirectly through the co-operative system (otherwise than by subscription to bonds and debenture issues) provided a certificate from the State Co-operative Bank/State Cooperative Agriculture and Rural

Development Bank (SCARDB), as the case may be, is produced, certifying the end use of such loans.

11. Investments by banks in special bonds issued by NABARD with the objective of financing exclusively agriculture/allied activities (not eligible for classification under priority sector lending with effect from April 1, 2007).
12. Loans for construction and running of storage facilities (warehouse, market yards, godowns, and silos), including cold storage units designed to store agriculture produce/products irrespective of their location.
13. If the storage unit is registered as SSI unit, the loans granted to such units may be classified under advances to SSI, provided the investment in plant and machinery is within the stipulated ceiling.
14. Advances to custom Service Units managed by individuals, institutions or organizations who maintain a fleet of tractors, bulldozers, well-boring equipment, threshers, combines, etc., and undertake work for farmers on contract basis.
15. Finance extended to dealers in drip irrigation/sprinkler irrigation system/agricultural machinery, irrespective of their location, subject to the following conditions:

- The dealer should be dealing exclusively in such items or if dealing in other products, should be maintaining separate and distinct records in respect of such items.
- Ceiling of up to ₹ 30 lakh per dealer should be observed.

16. Loans to Arthias (commission agents in rural/semi-urban areas functioning in markets/mandies) for extending credit to farmers, for supply of inputs as also for buying the output from the individual farmers/SHGs/JLGs.
17. Fifty percent of the credit outstanding under loans for general purposes under General Credit Cards (GCC).
18. Loans already disbursed and outstanding as on the date of this circular, to State Electricity Boards (SEBs) and power distribution corporations/companies, emerging out of

bifurcation/restructuring of SEBs, for reimbursing the expenditure already incurred by them for providing low tension connection from step-down point to individual farmers for energizing their wells and for Systems Improvement Scheme under Special Project Agriculture (SI-SPA), are eligible for classification as indirect finance up to March 2009.

The RBI also issued guidelines relating to the following:

1. Penalties for non-achievement of priority sector lending target/sub target.
2. Processing of application.
   - Issue of acknowledgment of application forms.
   - Disposal of application.
   - Rejection of proposals.
   - Register of rejected applications.
3. Repayment schedule.
4. Rates of Interest.
5. Penal interest.
6. Service charges/inspection charges.
7. Insurance against fire and other risks.
8. Current assets.
9. Discretionary Powers.
10. Capacity Building of the staff.
11. Machinery to look into complaints.

The banks should follow the above guideline prescribed by Reserve Bank for all categories of advances under the priority sector.

Conclusion

As the agriculture is the backbone of the Indian economy, agriculture credit is a nucleus of the system of farm operation. The RBI formulates guidelines to lending institutions regarding financing of priority sector, targets/sub-targets.

Agricultural credit through institutional channel is the only way to break agriculture stagnating. Even though some problems are associated with agriculture finance, the adequate and timely credit to the cultivators is vital and indispensable for the rehabilitation and progress of agriculturists.

10

Agriculture and Rural Banking

Ashish K. Makwana

Indian Agriculture

India is an agricultural country and agriculture is the main stay of Indian economy. Indian agriculture has achieved tremendous progress from the era of food shortages and imports to self sufficiency and exports. It is transformed from subsistence farming to intensive and technology led cultivation. Agriculture is considered as the backbone of Indian economy and is at the core of socio economic development of the country. Growth of other sectors of economy is dependent on agricultural growth to a great extent as it acts as a source of livelihood and food security for most of the rural households and is very significant for low income, poor and vulnerable sections of the society. Indian agriculture has passed through different phases. Each phase witnessed different policy changes. The pre green revolution period from 1950-51 till mid-1960s witnessed institutional changes, formidable agrarian reforms, growth of irrigation projects, removal of intermediary landlordism, imposition of land ceiling etc.

During the second phase of green revolution, agricultural policy was directed to attain food security through agrarian reforms. During this phase more focus was on research, extension, input supply, credit, marketing, price support, technology growth etc. After 1991, agriculture sector was also influenced by liberalization policies of Indian government. Agriculture was influenced by World Trade Organization (WTO) policies. It saw the opening up of domestic markets, deregulation, lesser government participation etc and called for more competitiveness in the sector and raised numerous challenges and opportunities.

India has made tremendous progress in agricultural field after independence and specifically in last three decades. The credit for this achievement goes to large number of small farmers which forms the backbone of India's agricultural economy. Policy support, production strategies, infrastructure investment, research and extension activities etc have also helped to increase food grain production. Higher agriculture production coupled with industrial growth have reduced the poverty but India has higher population pressure on land and other resources to meet its food development needs.

To meet the projected demand in the year 2020, India must obtain per hectare yield of 3.1 tons of wheat, 2.7 tons of rice, 1.3 tons of coarse cereals, 2.1 tons of maize, 1.3 tons of pulses, 2.4 tons of cereals, 25.7 tons of vegetables, 22.3 tons of potato, and 24.1 tons of fruits. The agriculture policy must accelerate all round development and economic viability of agriculture in comprehensive terms. Farmers must be provided the necessary support, encouragement and incentives. It must focus both on income and greater in farm and off farm job and livelihood opportunities. The investment that are good for agricultural growth, technology and its dissemination, rural infrastructure, education and irrigation act as a win-win strategy for decreasing rural poverty by increasing the non farm economy and increasing wages in rural areas.

The public investment in agriculture is reducing leading to decrease in productivity and low capital formation in agriculture sector. It is necessary to reverse this trend of productivity decline due to lack of investment. Private investment in agriculture is also at low level which is required to be stimulated by appropriate policies.

As 70 percent of population still lives in villages, agricultural growth will remain engine of broad based economic growth and development apart from food security and poverty alleviation. As small farmers play an important positive role in food security and poverty alleviation, development efforts must be aimed at the needs and potential of such farmers through their active participation in the growth process.

Although small farmers are most insecure and vulnerable group in the society, their contribution in securing foods for growing population have increased enormously. It was expected that in liberalized era, the non-agricultural employment in rural areas will increase. But this has not happened. More emphasis is to be placed on non-farm employment and necessary financial allocation and credit to rural people by banking system should be in place to promote rural enterprises.

Increasing the agricultural productivity needs continuous investment in human resource development, research and development in agriculture, improved information and extension, market, roads and related infrastructure development, farmer controlled irrigation technologies, etc. which would enable small farmers to adjust and respond to market conditions. Labour force is major endowment for economically weaker farm households. Economic growth with equity will provide increased entitlement through favourable markets for its products and higher employment opportunities.

If economic growth is not managed properly, it will give rise to inequalities in the society. Agrarian reforms to remove unequal access to land, water, credit facility, markets are must which will reduce inequalities and lead to increase in productivity.

Banking in India

India has very long tradition of banking. Vedic literature of 2000 to 1400 B.C mentions prevalence of money lending operations. Archaeological discoveries and Buddhist literature "Jatakas" mentions the existence of seethes or bankers. "Manu", the ancient law giver has also laid down many laws/rules regarding money transactions based upon gender and caste.

Indian banking sector has passed through several phases. The first phase started after nationalization of India's major 14 commercial banks in 1969. In this phase, nationalized banks tried to mop up new rural liquidity. The banks adopted social and development banking with the following objectives.

1. To make services of banks available in unbanked or under banked areas.
2. To extend enough credit to specific activities including agriculture.
3. To extend credit to disadvantageous group, viz. dalits and other poor households.

This was an early phase of green revolution. The farmers adopted new farming practices. In this phase rural banking witnessed growth in credit advances for agriculture. During this period a target of 40 percent of advances for agriculture/allied activities and small-scale and cottage industries was fixed for commercial banks.

The second phase began in late 1970s and 1980s. In this phase, land reform policy was discarded by the ruling classes themselves. Two important anti poverty schemes were launched: loan cum subsidy scheme for rural poor and state sponsored rural employment scheme. In this phase a very important scheme, namely integrated rural development programme was launched with the aim of creating productive income bearing assets among the rural poor by providing subsidized credit.

In 1991, India adopted the policy of liberalization. The third phase began with this liberalized era. In this era a committee on financial system was formed headed by M. Narasimham. The committee recommended that redistributive objectives should use the instrumentality of the fiscal rather than credit system and accordingly proposed that directed credit programmes should be phased out, interest rates be deregulated, capital adequacy norms be changed to compete with banks globally, branch licensing policy be revoked, new institutional structure which is market driven and based on profitability be created, part played by private Indian and foreign banks be enlarged.

Thus, the committee recommendation emphasize that banking policy be guided largely by the market force then by rules and regulation of public authority. The recommendations were not attempted to bring rural banking close to the poor but to throw the entire structure of social and development banking over board. The third phase inevitably witnessed reduction in rural banking in general and priority sector lending and preferential lending to the poor in particular.

Rural Banking Initiatives

The Reserve Bank of India (RBI) is given a mandate to closely involve in matter related to rural credit and banking as per Section 54 of RBI Act. As part of this mandate, All India Rural Credit Survey was undertaken in 1951-1952. The survey made agency wise estimates of rural indebtedness and found that cooperation has failed. Therefore, efforts were made on developing and strengthening cooperative credit structure. In 1955, State Bank of India (SBI) Act was enacted with the objective of extension of banking facilities on a large scale and particularly in rural and semi-urban areas. In 1969, 14 major commercial banks were nationalized which became important instruments for advancement of rural banking in addition to cooperatives and SBI. In 1975, regional rural banks were established in different states with equity participation from commercial banks, central and state governments. In 1982, NABARD was established to consolidate various arrangements provided by RBI to promote or supervise institutions and channel credit to rural areas.

Thus, several measures were undertaken to increase the flow of institutional credits for agriculture and rural lending. There were mismatches in credit and agricultural production. Field studies were performed to investigate the reasons and it was found that absence of local level planning was one of the reasons. In order to overcome the problem it was felt that with the establishment of large network of branches, a system could be allowed to allocate specific areas to each bank branch so as to concentrate on a focussed lending. To implement this idea, 'Service area approach' for commercial bank was implemented by RBI. The financial sector reforms initiated in1991 aimed at transforming the credit institutions into organizationally strong, financially viable and officially viable units. In order to achieve this following measures were introduced: Reduction of budgetary support and concessionality of resources, preparation of development action plans and signing of memoranda of understanding with major controllers, introduction of prudential norms relating to income recognition and asset classification for Regional Rural Banks (RRBs) and co-operative banks, deregulation of lending rates for this institutions, non target group financing for RRBs, direct financing for SCBs and CCBs. All this measures made many RRBs vibrant.

Some of the other policy measures for rural banking are additional capital contribution to National Bank for Agriculture and Rural Development (NABARD) by the RBI and Government of India, recapitalization and restructuring of RRBs, simplification of lending procedures, preparation of special credit plans by public sector banks and launching Kisan credit cards.

All these measures have led to a very wide network of rural financial institutions, development of banking culture, preparation of formal credit to rural areas and a counter to the dominance of money lenders. It has led to modernization of rural economies and implementation of anti poverty and self employment programmes.

Present Rural Credit Scenario

With opening up of economy in liberalised era since 1991, the Indian rural sector has also witnessed dramatic changes.

The importance of service sector has increased in rural areas also. The growth of cable television operators and its associated impact on rural life style is relevant example. Fulfilling the credit need of this sector is important. The integration between rural and urban areas is occurring at very fast pace. This has resulted in increase mobility of labour, capital, product and even credit between the two. Commercialization of agriculture has resulted in emergence of suppliers and buyers credits.

Thus, pesticides, fertilizer and many other inputs are provided to rural farmer on credit generally on deferred payment basis. Commission agents also advance money to farmer towards purchase of output as forward trading scheme. The formal banking transaction does not permit such credit facility. Due to commercialization of agriculture in some of the areas, traditional landlord based tenancy is replaced with commercial based tenancy. In such commercial based tenancy intensive cultivation of cash crops like cotton is adopted. The credit and banking facilities are not fully favourable to meet the working capital need of such commercial based tenancy. Rural agricultural has diversified in terms of product and process and one can see the growth of dairy, fish farms, horticultural along with different agricultural crops.

Due to unlimited wants of human beings, many rural people also adopt multiple tasks e.g. a small farmer acting as a petty trader and cable television operator in the area. This poses difficulty in end use specification and monitoring of credit. The commercialization is not even across the country. One can see prosperous farmers of Punjab and poor farmer of many tribal belts of the country. Norms and credit procedures are required to be different.

Informal finance: Although government has expanded the facilities of formal rural support institutes in the form of banks, informal financial market is outside the orbit of officially regulated financial intermediaries. There are three types of informal financial transaction, viz. well defined group, tied lending/borrowing untied lending/borrowing activities. Historically, the informal debt market has been equated with either landlord or moneylender. It is said that there are often unequal and exploitative arrangements between rural poor (farmers) and the moneylender and as they are unregulated, prima facia they are not desirable.

However, the fact is that informal debt markets do exist and research studies have shown that in some parts of the country it account for more than 50 percent of debt transactions. In informal debt market, transaction costs in terms of certainty, timeliness, procedural requirement, number of trips etc is negligible. Informal market caters to more risky borrowings then formal markets. Directed credit, high reserve ratio, interest rate ceiling, and branch licensing etc. make informal financial market popular and attractive.

Technological development and rural banking: The role of banks have changed over a period of years. Now a days they perform variety of functions in the form of saving and disbursing loans in different forms. They provide services such as investment, merchant banking, insurance products etc, Banks try to increase their customer base by going into the rural areas, launching schemes such as opening account even with zero balance. The emergence and growth of Automated Teller Machine (ATMs) have increased the customer convenience without physical direct contact to the semi urban area. ATM has now penetrated up to rural areas. Another noteworthy development is about popularity of credit cards which are bound to reach rural areas.

Problems of Rural Credit

Rural people need financial support for many purposes. They need it to meet short term requirements of working capital and for long term investment in agriculture and other income bearing activities. As agricultural activities are seasonal, rural people need financial support to balance seasonal fluctuations in earning and expenditure. Apart from agricultural needs, rural households also need financial support to meet different types of consumptions (food, housing, health, education) and to meet social obligations and customs.

The burden of indebtedness in rural India is great which mainly falls on the rural working people. Many structural changes in credit institutions/rural banks, ways of rural credit have been implemented after independence in India. But still farmers are exploited in the credit market. This finally results in 'farmer suicides' in extreme cases. Such suicide instances support the statement that 'Indian peasant is born in debt, lives in debt and dies in debt'. This statement represents true picture of many rural working people.

Historically, rural credits have encountered many problems. This problem can be classified into two categories.

1. **Rural Individual Problems:** Supply of formal sector credit is inadequate, rural credit market have been imperfect and fragmented, formal sector credit has been unequal in respect of region, class, caste and gender, major source of credit still remains to be informal sector loans with high interest rates.
2. **Organizational Problems:** The co-operative banks have different layers and many co-operative banks have large non performing assets. The cost of financial intermediation by various rural financial institutions is considered to be on high side. Institutional credit is generally more likely to be available for well to do among the rural population. Non-availability of timely credit and the cumbersome procedure for obtaining credit is result of poor functioning of financial institutions.

Strategies

1. The policy of rural banking should aim at enhancing the supply of credit in rural financial markets by enlarging the coverage of directly disbursed credit by formal sector.
2. Decreasing true cost of credit availability to rural areas.
3. Undertake procedural simplification.

4. Expand the activities from delivery of credit to rural people to make available financial services and products to investors and consumers in villages.

References

Ramachandran, V.K and Madhura Swaminathan. 'Does Informal Credit Provide Security? Rural Banking Policy in India' http://www.ilo.org/ses.

Reddy, Y.V. 'Future of Rural Banking' www.rbidocs.rbi.org.in/rdocs/Bulletin/PDFs/10991.pdf.

11

Financial Inclusion of Rural Poor in India

P. Adi Lakshmi, Rajesh C. Jampala and Srinivasa Rao Dokku

Introduction

According to RBI estimates, there are over 450 million "unbanked people" in India, most of whom live in rural areas. The term "unbanked" refers to people who have no access to formal financial services, but rather must rely on either family, or informal providers of finance, such as the village moneylender. It is undisputed that access to finance is critical for enabling individuals and communities to climb out of poverty. It is also generally agreed that relying on the limited resources of village moneylenders exposes the poor to coercive lending practices, personal risks and high interest rates, which can be a much as150 percent.

NSSO data reveal that 45.9 million farmer households in the country (51.4 percent), out of a total of 89.3 million households do not access credit, either from institutional or non-institutional sources. Further, despite the vast network of bank branches, only 27 percent of total farm households are indebted to formal sources (of which one-third also borrow from informal sources). Farm households not accessing credit from formal sources as a proportion to total farm households is especially high at 95.91 percent, 81.26 percent and 77.59 percent in the North Eastern, Eastern and Central Regions respectively. Thus, apart from the fact that exclusion in general is large, it also varies widely across regions, social groups and asset holdings. The poorer the group, the greater is the exclusion.

Successive Indian governments have tried to alleviate financial exclusion by requiring the formal sector to provide services to low-income households or to certain economic sector. Banks must lend at least 40 percent of their total assets to mandated priority sector, including 18 percent to agriculture, and required to provide such as no-frill accounts to households. If India keeps to its current course, its rate of financial inclusion will improve slightly because of the changing distribution of households by income. From 2006 through 2010, India's population is forecast to grow around 80 million people, or 16 million households. Most of households will still be clustered in the bottom income tiers, but the size of poorest tier will decline. The middle income tiers will grow the most.

Meaning of Financial Inclusion

The definition of financial inclusion currently in use is the delivery of financial services at an affordable cost to vast sections of disadvantaged and low-income groups. Financial services include the provision of savings, loans, insurance, payments and remittance facilities by the formal financial system to those who tend to be excluded. Given the above context, to truly financially include the poor would require creating a variety of risk/vulnerability management mechanisms and ensuring that they are consistently and simultaneously available. Unless major risks are simultaneously covered, the likelihood of one risk wiping out an entire livelihood is a very high possibility, and people who have been temporarily included would be excluded again. Take the example of low income groups engaged in agriculture. As renowned journalist P. Sainath often argues, bankers/MFIs are not going to give out fresh loans after they have overdues. 'They know that small/marginal farmers, who could not pay back ₹ 10,000 earlier, cannot repay ₹ 20,000 now. And the more the (formal) banking system denies the farmer aid, the more he must go to the *sahukar*'.

History of Financial Inclusion in India

Financial inclusion, in the broadest meaning of the term, has been an area of concern for the financial policymakers, regulators and the Government of India ever since Independence. Some of the major landmarks during the last half-century of the second millennium were:

1. In 1954, the All-Indian Rural Survey Committee recommended the creation of a State-sponsored bank to promote rural penetration. Based on these recommendations the State Bank of India was established in 1955.
2. 14 major commercial banks were nationalized in July 1969. The Lead Bank Scheme was launched in 1970 for developing and implementing district-focused banking plans.
3. Regional Rural Banks came into being in 1976 with the objective of blending the skills of commercial banks with the knowledge that the co-operatives possessed about the rural economy.
4. In 1980, six more commercial banks were nationalized.
5. NABARD was established in 1982 as an apex institution to formulate policies and plans oversee operations in the field of agricultural credit and rural development.
6. The first SHG-Bank Linkage Programme was launched in 1992, which gathered momentum from 1999 onwards.

Nationalization of banks in 1969 transformed the banking industry beyond recognition. Branch networks of the banks grew significantly reaching across the entire country and the nation saw banking being taken to the masses. Almost two and a half decades of directed, production-based, subsidized social lending were witnessed. Towards the end of this phase, the economy began to buckle under the strain of internal inefficiencies and external pressures. The early 1990s saw major reforms being implemented to shore up the national economy and banking. By the end of the decade, stability had been restored and the first few years of the 21st century had seen the economy on a growth path.

During the period after nationalization, the number of bank branches has grown twelve-fold from 8,262 in 1969 to 99,523 as at the end-March 2011. With the rapid spread of branch networks of banks, the number of customers per branch declined fourfold from 64,000 in 1969 to 15,000. Thus, in effect, the coverage in terms of total number of customers has more than doubled. However, during this period, the total population of the country also doubled (0.55 billion as per the 1971 Census to 1.20 billion as per the 2011 Census).

This implies that despite the phenomenal expansion of bank branches across the country, the extent of financial exclusion of bank branches across the country, i.e. the proportion of the population that has no access to basic banking services has not reduced significantly since 1969.

Extent of Financial Exclusion in India

To understand the financial inclusion better it is better to look at exactly the opposite of financial inclusion, i.e., financial exclusion. Broadly defined, financial exclusion signifies the lack of access by certain segments of the society to appropriate, low-cost, fair and safe financial products and services from mainstream providers. Financial exclusion is thus a key policy concern, because the options for operating a household budget, or a micro/small enterprise, without mainstream financial services can often be expensive. This process becomes self-reinforcing and can often be an important factor in social exclusion, especially for communities with limited access to financial products, particularly in rural areas. The following are the main reasons for financial exclusion in India:

1. Precursor programmes with a strong microfinance component do not exist.
2. Difficult terrain to cover.
3. Microfinance methodology is unsuitable.
4. Inappropriate microfinance products.

5. Strong government support is not available.
6. Remoteness is high.
7. Illiteracy is a problem.
8. Poor infrastructure.
9. Poor social infrastructure.
10. Fewer bank branches.
11. Greater average distance from branch.
12. Unsuitable branch timings.
13. Cumbersome documentation.
14. Difficult procedures.
15. Strong dependence on agriculture livelihoods.
16. Lack of diversified livelihoods and non-farm work.
17. Irregular branch timings.
18. Large number of excluded groups.
19. Large number of poor.
20. Self-exclusion from SHGs/MFIs for various reasons.

State-wise Financial Exclusion in India

The analysis of financial exclusion according to geographical spread provided in the Table 11.1 revealed that in 7 states (i.e. Arunachal Pradesh, Assam, Jharkhand, Manipur, Meghalaya, Mizoram and Uttaranchal,) more than 75 percent farmer households were found to be financially excluded on the other hand, exclusion was relatively low in southern states. Whereas in other states like Madhya Pradesh, Maharashtra, Punjab, Rajasthan and West Bengal the financial exclusion is in the range of 25 percent to 50 percent. Andhra Pradesh ranks best in terms of financial inclusion among all states in the country.

Financial Inclusion Statistics in India

General:

1. 51.4 percent of farmer households are financially excluded from both formal/informal sources.
2. Of the total farmer households, only 27 percent access formal sources of credit; one third of this group also

borrow from non-formal sources.

3. Overall, 73 percent of farmer households have no access to formal sources of credit. Only 13 percent are availing loans from the banks in the income bracket of less than ₹ 50,000.
4. 53 percent people are taking loans from the institutional and non-institutional sources only for emergency purposes
5. Critical Exclusion in terms of credit is manifest in 256 districts across 17 states and 1 UT (Dadra and Nagar Haveli).
6. Even rich people are excluded and have to depend on non-institutional sources for loan purposes.

Table 11.1: Extent of Financial Exclusion–State-wise

Extent of Financial exclusion	States
Above 75 percent	Meghalaya, Arunachal Pradesh, Uttarakhand, Assam, Mizoram, Manipur, Jharkhand.
50 percent to 75 percent	Bihar, Chatisgarh, Himachal Pradesh, Jammu & Kashmir, Nagaland, Orissa, Sikkim, Tripura, Uttar Pradesh.
25 percent to 50 percent	Karnataka, Kerala, Madhya Pradesh, Maharashtra, Punjab, Rajasthan, Tamil Nadu, West Bengal.
Below 25 percent	Andhra Pradesh

Source: www.ficci.com.

Region-wise:

1. Exclusion is most acute in Central, Eastern and North-Eastern regions—having a concentration of 64 percent of all financially excluded farmer households in the country.
2. Overall indebtedness to formal sources of finance alone is only 19.66 percent in these three regions.

Occupational Groups:

1. Marginal farmer households constitute 66 percent of total farm households. Only 45 percent of these households are

indebted to either formal or non-formal sources of finance.

2. About 20 percent of indebted marginal farmer households have access to formal sources of credit.
3. Among non-cultivator households nearly 80 percent do not access credit from any source.

Social Groups:

1. Only 36 percent of ST farmer households are indebted [SCs and Other Backward Classes (OBC)-51 percent] mostly to informal sources.
2. Analysis of the data provided by RBI thru' its Basic Statistical Returns reveal that critical exclusion (in terms of credit) is manifest in 256 districts, spread across 17 States and 1 UT, with a credit gap of 95 percent and above. This is in respect of commercial banks and RRBs.

Inclusion of Financially Excluded

The Expert Group on Agricultural Indebtedness (July, 2007) recommended that the main focus of the programme of 'financial inclusion' should be on the basis of credit needs of all small borrower households. Institutional credit should be extended to those excluded farmer households who do not have access to any source of credit.

This coverage should be placed on a mission mode for the farm community as a part of the strategy of financial inclusion and as a part of the goal of mitigating distress amongst the farming community. This should involve institutions like-scheduled commercial banks, Regional Rural Banks (RRBs) and cooperatives, and through them, agencies like business facilitators and business correspondents.

In November 2005, banks were advised to make available a basic banking 'no-frills' account with low or nil minimum stipulated balances as well as charges to expand the outreach of such accounts to vast sections of the population. Several banks have since introduced such 'no-frills' account with and without value-added features. According to the information available with the Reserve Bank, about five lakh no-frill accounts have been opened until March 31, 2006, of which about two-third are with the public sector and one-third with the private sector banks.

In order to ensure that persons belonging to low income group, both in urban and rural areas do not encounter difficulties in opening bank accounts owing to procedural hassles, the know your customer (KYC) procedures for opening accounts has been simplified. The Reserve Bank has directed banks to make available all printed material used by retail customers in English, Hindi and the concerned regional language. More recently, in January 2006, banks were permitted to utilise the services of non-governmental organisations (NGOs/SHGs), micro-finance institutions and other civil society organisations as intermediaries in providing financial and banking services through the use of business facilitator and business correspondent models.

To extend hassle-free credit to bank customers in rural areas, the guidelines on general credit card (GCC) schemes were simplified to enable customers' access credit on simplified terms and conditions, without insistence on security, purpose or end-use of credit. With a view of providing hassle free credit to customers, banks were allowed to issue general credit cards akin to Kisan Credit Cards. A simplified mechanism for one-time settlement of loans with principal amount up to ₹ 25,000, which have become doubtful and loss assets as on September 30, 2005, was suggested for adoption. In case of loans granted under Government-sponsored schemes, banks were advised to frame separate guidelines following a state-specific approach to be evolved by the State-Level Bankers' Committee (SLBC). Banks have been specifically advised that borrowers with loans settled under the one time settlement scheme will be eligible to re-access the formal financial system for fresh credit. Banks were advised to give effect to these measures at all branches for achieving greater financial inclusion. Initiatives have also been undertaken towards achieving greater financial inclusion in the

North-Eastern Region, which had perennially remained under banked.

Government Programmes for Financial Inclusion

SHG-Bank Linkage Scheme: The SHG-Bank Linkage Programme can be regarded as the most potent initiative since Independence for delivering financial services to the poor in a sustainable manner. The SHG-Bank linkage thus, took birth and is the talk of the walk. The bank linkage program allowed the rural poor, a group often ignored by the traditional banking sector, access to mainstream financing. Throughout the decade, NABARD was able to link 1.5 million SHGs (cumulative) to banks (NABARD) with ₹ 6.8 billion of loan amount by March 2005. There were more than 69.53 lakh savings linked SHGs and more than 48.51 lakh credit linked SHGs covering 9.7 crore poor households as on 31 March 2011, under the microfinance programme.

Micro Finance Programme: Micro-finance has been another important component of the financial inclusion process in India. Micro-finance is defined as provision of thrift, credit and financial services and products of very small amount to the poor in rural, semi-urban and urban areas for enabling them to raise their income levels and improving living standards. The Self-Help Group-Bank Linkage Programme (SBLP), which started as a pilot programme in 1992 has developed with rapid strides over the years. In 2009-10, 1.59 million new SHGs were credit-linked with banks, and bank loan of ₹ 14,453 crore (including repeat loan) was disbursed to these SHGs.

No-frills Accounts: The Central Bank has made concerted efforts since 2004 to promote financial inclusion. Accordingly, to expand the outreach of banking services to vast sections of the population, banks, in November 2005, were advised to make available a basic 'no-frills' account with low or nil balances as well as charges. Following this, several banks have introduced 'no-frills' accounts. Between end-March 2006 and end-March 2007, about 33,024,761 new 'no-frills' bank accounts were opened. Public sectors banks accounted for bulk of these new 'no-frills' accounts due to their vast branch network in rural and semi-urban areas. Financial inclusion is being viewed by these banks as a huge business opportunity in rural and semi-urban areas in an environment of intense competition.

Kisan Credit Cards (KCCs): The Kisan Credit Card (KCC) Scheme, introduced in 1998 for timely and hassle-free short term loans has been extended to borrowers for term credit and consumption loans as well. As on October 31st 2011, 1078.36 lakh KCCs had been issued by the banking system. Of the total 1078.36 lakh cards issued, the commercial banks accounted for the largest share of 45 percent followed by co-operative banks (39 percent) and Regional Rural Banks (15 percent). Joint studies conducted by NABARD and the financing banks on implementation of the KCC Scheme have confirmed that the Scheme was well received both by farmers and bankers and the flexibility in operations has resulted in improved loan recoveries. The KCC scheme is being implemented by cooperative banks, commercial banks and RRBs. By the end of October 31, 2011, a total amount of ₹ 5,27,052 crore has been sanctioned under KCCs.

Micro Insurance: Micro-insurance is a key element in the financial services package for people at the bottom of the pyramid. The poor face more risks than the well off. It is becoming increasingly clear that micro-insurance needs a further push and guidance from the Regulator as well as the Government. The Committee concurs with the view that offering micro credit without micro-insurance is self-defeating. There is, therefore, a need to emphasis linking of micro credit with micro-insurance. The country has moved on to a higher growth trajectory. To sustain and accelerate the growth momentum, we have to ensure increased participation of the economically weak segments of population in the process of economic growth. Financial inclusion of hitherto excluded segments of population is a critical part of this process of inclusion. We hope that the recommendations made in this

Report, if implemented, will accelerate the process of financial inclusion.

Financial Inclusion Fund (FIF): The Government of India had set up the Rangarajan Committee on Financial Inclusion (in June 2006) to look into the issues involved and suggest measures for bringing the excluded population into the ambit of financial system. The Committee envisaged that 50 percent of the excluded rural households (55.8 million) should have access to financial services by 2012, and the rest by2015. Towards this end, two funds recommended by the Committee, have been set up in NABARD, viz., 'Financial Inclusion Fund' (FIF) for meeting the cost of developmental and promotional interventions of financial inclusion and 'Financial Inclusion Technology Fund' (FITF), for meeting the cost of technology adoption. Each Fund consists of an overall corpus of ₹ 500 crore, to be contributed by the GoI, RBI and NABARD in the ratio of 40:40:20 in a phased manner over five years, depending upon utilisation of funds. GoI and NABARD made initial upfront contributions of ₹ 10 and ₹ 5 crore, respectively to each of these funds, for 2007-08. GoI again contributed ₹ 10 crore for 2009-10 to each of the funds. Reserve Bank of India has decided to contribute to the funds on reimbursement basis. Ason 31 March 2010, the total contribution under FIF and FITF stood at ₹ 50 crore each. The guidelines for these two funds have been formulated and circulated among stakeholders.

National Rural Financial Inclusion Plan: A National Rural Financial Inclusion Plan (NRFIP) may be launched with a clear target to provide access to comprehensive financial services, including credit, to at least 50 percent of financially excluded households, say 55.77 million by 2012 through rural/semi-urban branches of Commercial Banks and Regional Rural Banks. The remaining households, with such shifts as may occur in the rural/urban population, have to be covered by 2015. Semi-urban and rural branches of commercial banks and RRBs may set for themselves a minimum target of covering

250 new cultivator and non-cultivator households per branch per annum, with an emphasis on financing marginal farmers and poor non-cultivator households.

Development and Technology Funds: There is a cost involved in this massive exercise of extending financial services to hitherto excluded segments of population. Such costs may come down over a period of time with the resultant business expansion. However, in the initial stages some funding support is required for promotional and developmental initiatives that will lead to better credit absorption capacity among the poor and vulnerable sections and for application of technology for facilitating the mandated levels of inclusion. The Committee has, therefore, proposed the constitution of two funds with NABARD–the Financial Inclusion Promotion and Development Fund and the Financial Inclusion Technology Fund with an initial corpus of ₹ 500 crore each to be contributed in equal proportion by GoI/RBI/NABARD. This recommendation has already been accepted by GoI.

Swarozgar Credit Card Scheme: The scheme was introduced by NABARD in 2003 for facilitating hassle-free availability of credit for meeting investment and working capital requirements of small borrowers/micro-entrepreneurs. During the year, 2.11 lakh cards were issued with a credit limit of ₹ 756.90 crore. As on 31st March 2007, 98 RRBs, 43 commercial banks and 138 co-operative banks had introduced the scheme and issued 6.79 lakh cards involving credit limits of ₹ 2,700 crore. Under the pilot scheme introduced during 2005-06 for supporting select RRBs and co-operative banks with one-time grant assistance for promoting the Swarozgar Credit Card (SCC) scheme, 12 banks have been sanctioned grant assistance of ₹ 11.58 lakh.

Joint Liability Groups (JLGs): SHG-bank linkage has emerged as an effective credit delivery channel to the poor clients. However, there are segments within the poor such as share croppers/oral lessees/tenant farmers, whose loan requirements are much larger but who have no collaterals to fit into the traditional financing approaches of the banking system. To service such clients, Joint Liability Groups (JLGs), an upgradation of SHG model, could be an effective way. NABARD had piloted a project for formation and linking of JLGs during 2004-05 in 8 States of the country through 13 RRBs. Based on the encouraging response from the project, a scheme for financing JLGs of tenant farmers and oral lessees has also been evolved. The Committee has recommended that adoption of the JLGs concept could be another effective method for purveying credit to mid-segment clients such as small farmers, marginal farmers, tenant farmers, etc. and thereby reduce their dependence on informal sources of credit.

Micro Finance Development and Equity Fund (MFDEF): The Micro-finance Development and Equity Fund (MFDEF) is being utilised for promotion of various microfinance activities such as formation and linkage of SHGs through SHPIs, training and capacity building of stake holders, capital and soft loan assistance to MFIs, livelihood propagation, studies, documentation, etc. During 2009-10, an amount of ₹ 80.91 crore was released, of which ₹ 20.49 crore was grant support for promotional activities and ₹ 60.42 crore was for Capital Support/Revolving Fund Assistance (RFA) to MFIs, as against ₹ 18.73 crore and ₹ 15.93 crore in the previous year, respectively.

Role of RRBs in Financial Inclusion

RRBs, post-merger, represent a powerful instrument for financial inclusion. Their outreach vis-à-vis other scheduled commercial banks particularly in regions and across population groups facing the brunt of financial exclusion is impressive. RRBs account for 37 percent of total rural offices of all scheduled commercial banks and 91 percent of their workforce is posted in rural and semi-urban areas. They account for 31 percent of deposit accounts and 37 percent of loan accounts in rural areas. RRB's have a large presence in regions marked by financial exclusion of a high order. They account for 34 percent of all branches in North-Eastern, 30 percent in Eastern and 32 percent in Central regions. Out of the total 22.38 lakh SHGs credit linked by the banking industry as on 31st March 2006, 33 percent of the linkages were by RRBs which is quite impressive to say the least. Significantly the more backward the region the greater is the share of RRBs which is amply demonstrated by their 56 percent share in the North-Eastern, 48 percent in Central and 40 percent in Eastern region.

Role of Commercial Banks in Financial Inclusion

Commercial banks play a pivotal role in financial inclusion initiatives. The survey carried out by the World Bank in 142 economies reveals that 85 percent of total deposit volume and 96 percent of all deposit accounts are held in commercial banks. But, in a number of economies, non-banking institutions play an important role in providing basic deposit services. For example, in countries like Chile, Spain, and France, cooperatives or specialized state financial institutions hold more deposit accounts than commercial banks. Similarly, in a number of West African countries, such as Benin, Burkina Faso, Ivory Coast, and Niger, deposit-taking microfinance institutions have more depositors than commercial banks, suggesting that non-banking institutions can play an important role in providing basic deposit services.

Revitalising the Cooperative System

Though the network of commercial banks and RRBs has spread rapidly and they now have nearly 50,000 rural/semi-urban branches, their reach in the countryside both in terms of the number of clients and accessibility to the small and marginal farmers and other poorer segments is far less than that of cooperatives. In terms of number of agricultural credit accounts, the Short Term Cooperative Credit System (STCCS) has 50 percent more accounts than the commercial banks and RRBs put together. On an average, there is one PACS for every 6 villages; these societies have a total membership of more than 120 million rural people making it one of the largest rural financial systems in the world. However, the health of a very large proportion of these rural credit cooperatives has deteriorated significantly.

To achieve universal access, new banking systems are needed that work for the poor and yet are commercially sustainable. What poor people need is: first, convenience, being able to transact near where they live and work; second, trust, putting their money with organizations that seem to care for them and who they feel are going to be there for them when they need them the most; and third, affordability, being able to transact in small amounts at reasonable cost.

To be successful at mobilizing savings of poor people, three key aspects need to be addressed:

1. **Distribution.** Customers are not willing to travel far or wait long in queues to save relatively meagre balances. Each village and neighbourhood where poor people live ought to have a transactional point where cash can be converted into electronic value (and vice versa).
2. **Brand.** Customers need to feel that their money is safe, yet they are often in no position to ascertain the financial condition of financial institutions. They also need to feel like they are welcome and their interests are being protected.
3. **Products**. In order to adopt formal savings, the poor must be offered a ladder of savings-related benefits. There is a saving chasm between the short-term, informal saving they do today and the longer-term, formal saving that would be most impact in their lives.

Technology can be used to ensure that banks and their customers interact remotely in a totally trusted way through local retail outlets. This requires that: (i) customers be properly authenticated (for instance using cards or their mobile phones), (ii) customers transactions must be undertaken against the store's own bank account (so that stores in effect 'prepay' customers' deposits), and (iii) transactions are authorized and recorded in real time by the bank (using point of sale terminals or mobile phones to communicate with the bank).

With the spread of mobile communications networks, all this can happen in real time, in which case there is minimal credit risk: the transaction is done and settled by the time the customer walks out of the door, and the store's cash is always the store's. There are an estimated 1 billion people in developing countries who have a mobile phone but not a bank account. In Africa alone, 50 percent of the population has cell phones, more than double the number of people who have access to bank accounts. With that alone we can go a long way to cracking the problem of getting bank accounts to the poor.

Conclusion

It is increasingly apparent that addressing financial exclusion will require a holistic approach on the part of the banks in creating awareness about financial products, education, and advice on money management, debt counselling, savings and affordable credit. Using new technologies, alternative distribution channels, and new partnerships everyone can have a safe place to save. We need to optimistic financial models that can transform the economics of financial service delivery, which will in turn give poor people more tools to manage their lives and plan paths out of poverty.

Reference

Amitabh Guha. *"Financial Inclusion: An Overview"*. Inclusive Growth A New Challenge, Bankers' Conference 2006.

ATISG (2010),*"Innovative Financial Inclusion"* principles and Report on innovative Financial Inclusion from the access Through Innovation Sub-Group of the G20 Financial Inclusion, Experts Group, 25 May, 2010.

Doug Johnson and Sushmita Meka (2010) *"Access to Finance in Andhra Pradesh"* Institute for Financial Management and Research centre for Micro Finance, and Centre for Microfinance

Research Banks" Institute of Rural Development, October 2010.

Government of India. "II and III Periodic Report on the convention on the Elimination of all Forms of Discrimination Against Women". *CEDAW Periodic Report,* Government of India, 2005.

Ignacio Mas (2010) "*New Opportunities to Tackle the Challenge of Financial Inclusion*" Working Paper Series No. 40, Institute for Financial Management and Research, Centre for Micro Finance, August 2010.

Janmejayasinha and Arvind Subramanin. *"The Next Billion Customers A Road Map for Expanding Financial Inclusion in India"*. The Boston Consulting Group, November, 2007.

Jaya .S. Anand. "Self-help Groups in Empowering Women: Case Study of Selected SHGs and NHGs". *Kerala Research Programme on Local Level Development Centre for Development Studies,* Tiruvanthapuram, 2002.

Legatum Ventures (2011),*"Microfinance in India: a Crisis at the bottom of the pyramid"* Legatum ventures, May 2011.

Manimekalai. "Impact of various forms of micro financing on women". *Department of Women Child Development, Ministry of Human Resource Development*, Government of India, 2004.

Manimekalai. "*Impact of various forms of micro financing on women"*. Department of Women Child Development, Ministry of Human Resource Development, Government of India, 2004.

NABARD "Annual Report 2009-10.

Nabard "Status of Micro Finance in India–2009-10" *NABARD, Mumbai*, India.

Prabhu Ghate. "Micro Finance in India A State of the Sector Report, 2006". *FORD Foundation*, 2006.

Rajesh C. Jampala, Dr. Adi Lakshmi and Mr. Srinivasa Rao Dokku (2011),"Critical Evaluation of Thrust Areas in Agriculture Sector–A Way Forward" edited volume titled Engendering Agriculture Development: Emerging perspective, Issues, Challenges and Strategies" published by Novel Corporation, Chennai, June 2011, pp. 424-447.

Rajesh C. Jampala, Dr. Adi Lakshmi and Mr. Srinivasa Rao Dokku (2011),"Regulatory Issues in Micro Finance Sector–A Case study of Andhra Pradesh" published in Reference Book titled "Embodiment of Empowerment Self Help Groups" published by The Vijay Nicole Imprints Private Limited, Chennai, 2011, pp. 410-420.

Rajesh C. Jampala, Dr. Adi Lakshmi and Mr. Srinivasa Rao Dokku (2011),"Performance Evaluation of SHG-Bank Linkage Programme in India" published in Reference Book titled "Microfinance–Enabling Empowerment" (ISBN 10:81-8209-265-5) published by The Vijay Nicole Imprints Private Limited, Chennai.

Rakesh Mohan. *"Economic Growth, Financial Depending a Financial Inclusion"*. Reserve Bank of India, 2006.

Ramesh S. Arunachalam (2008),*"Scoping paper on Financial Inclusion Considerations and Recommendations for UNDP"* The United Nations Development Programme (UNDP), January, 2008.

Y.S.P. Thorat. *"Indian Banking: Shaping an Economic Powerhouse"*. www.ficci.com, 2006.

12

Regional Rural Banks (RRBs) in India

P. Adi Lakshmi, Rajesh C. Jampala and
Srinivasa Rao Dokku

Introduction

The institution of Regional Rural Banks (RRBs) was created to meet the excess demand for institutional credit in the rural areas, particularly among the economically and socially marginalised sections. Although the cooperative banks and the commercial banks had reasonable records in terms of geographical coverage and disbursement of credit, in terms of population groups the cooperative banks were dominated by the rural rich, while the commercial banks had a clear urban bias. In order to provide access to low-cost banking facilities to the poor, the Narasimham Working Group (1975) proposed the establishment of a new set of banks, as institutions which combine the local feel and the familiarity with rural problems which the cooperatives possess and the degree of business organization, ability to mobilize deposits, access to central money markets and modernized outlook which the commercial banks have.

The multi-agency approach to rural credit was also to serve the needs of the input-intensive agricultural strategy (Green Revolution) which had initially focused on `betting on the strong' but by the mid-seventies was ready to spread more widely through the Indian countryside. In addition, the potential and the need for diversification of economic activities in the rural areas had begun to be recognized, and this was a sector where the RRBs could play a meaningful role. The RRBs Act, 1976 succinctly sums up this overall vision to sub-serve both the developmental and the redistributive objectives:

The RRBs were established with a view to developing the rural economy by providing, for the purpose of development of agriculture, trade, commerce, industry and other productive activities in the rural areas, credit and other facilities, particularly to small and marginal farmers, agricultural labourers, artisans and small entrepreneurs, and for matters connected there with and incidental thereto.

For some time the RRBs performed well. But, their performance deteriorated during the 1990s. However, beginning with 2002, their performance has improved. During the 1990s their recovery rates were low, they had low earning capacity because of limits imposed on the interest rates they could charge, and there was a big increase in wages and salaries. Moreover, the sponsoring banks competed with them and ran their own branches in the area of operation of the RRBs. As a result, RRBs began to run into losses and most of them had large Non Performing Assets (NPAs). Several committees were set up to look into the problems of RRBs and suggest improvements. The Dantwala Committee recommended that RRBs should also finance non-target group borrowers. It did not favour the merger of RRBs with the sponsoring bank, as this would not solve the problem of losses but only conceal them.

Most other committees were concerned with improving the financial health of RRBs through capitalisation or through reorganisation (Working Group on RRBs, 1986; Agricultural Credit Review Committee, Khusro Committee, 1989; Committee on Financial System, Narasimham Committee, 1991; and Committee on Restructuring of RRBs, Bhandari Committee, 1994). Recently, the Advisory Committee on Flow of Credit to Agriculture and Related Activities from the Banking System, popularly known as Vyas Committee (2004) recommended that RRBs should continue but should be restructured into viable financial institutions, simultaneously retaining their regional character and rural focus. The reforms initiated in stages would ultimately result in 20 state-level

RRBs. RBI is also looking into the restructuring of RRBs.

Performance of RRBs in India

These changes were primarily reflected in the restructuring and amalgamation, recapitalisation of RRBs along with the application of prudential regulatory framework to these institutions. In 2009-10, the consolidated balance sheet of RRBs showed accelerated growth of 22.2 percent as compared to 16.5 percent during the previous year. On the liabilities side, deposits propelled the growth in balance sheets of RRBs, while on the assets side, the growth was mainly on account of investments. It may be noted that the credit-deposit ratio of RRBs in 2009-10 stood at 57.6 percent, a level far lower than that of SCBs (Table 12.1).

Out of 82 RRBs, 79 RRBs were in profits during 2009-10 indicating an increase in the share of profit-making RRBs to 96.3 percent during this year as compared to 93.0 percent in the previous year. On the whole, all RRBs taken together reported a net profit of ₹ 1,884 crore showing a growth of 41.1 percent in 2009-10. As a result, there was a marginal rise in the Return on Assets (RoA) of RRBs from 1.0 percent in 2008-09 to 1.1 percent in 2009-10. The RoA of RRBs in 2009-10 thus worked out to be relatively higher than that of SCBs.

Role and Performance of Rural Banks

Within the Indian financial sector, the role of the rural banks is important but not apparently pre-eminent. The contribution of the commercial banks to the rural/semi-urban banking network is far higher (at 38 percent of the total) than the 28 percent contribution of rural banks to the total of 87,000 bank branches in India. Despite the apparent importance of commercial banks even in the rural areas however they are neither able nor willing to serve the poorest sections of the population. By comparison, in the credit categories of direct relevance to financial inclusion, RRBs hold 26.2 percent of agricultural credit accounts and as many as 55.0 percent of all artisan/tiny industry loan accounts. This amounts to much lower proportions of overall credit available under these categories–just 10.9 percent and 11.0 percent respectively–since RRB loan sizes average just ₹ 25,000 and ₹ 13,000 for these two categories, much smaller than those offered by the commercial banks.

Table 12.1: Consolidated Balance Sheet of Regional Rural Banks, 2009-10 (Amount in ₹ crore)

Item	At end-March		Percentage variation
Share Capital	197	197	-
Reserves	6,754	8,065	19.4
Share Capital Deposits	3,959	3,985	0.7
Deposits	1,20,189	1,45,035	20.7
Current	6,432	8,065	25.4
Savings	63,675	75,906	19.2
Term	50,082	61,064	21.9
Borrowings from	12,735	18,770	47.4
NABARD	8,690	12,521	44.1
Sponsor Bank	3,931	6,165	56.8
Others	114	84	-26.3
Other Liabilities	6,820	8,041	17.9
Total Liabilities/Assets	1,50,654	1,84,093	22.2
Cash in Hand	1,587	1,784	12.4
Balances with RBI	5,882	8,145	38.5
Other Bank Balances	31,865	39,102	22.7
Investments	37,984	47,289	24.5
Loans and Advances (net)	65,609	79,157	20.6
Fixed Assets	278	379	36.3
Other Assets #	7,449	8,237	10.6
1 Credit -Deposit Ratio	56.4	57.6	-
2 Investment-Deposit Ratio	54.8	50.2	-
3 (Credit + Investment) -Deposit Ratio	111.3	107.8	-

Source: NABARD.

Yet, it is precisely this fact that shows the importance of the rural banks for otherwise financially excluded sections of the population. Low income families have a much lower absolute and proportionate need for credit than better off sections of the population that are, in any case, better able to access the commercial banks. Similar data for cooperatives is not available but with an estimated 130 million members the average loan outstanding with cooperatives amounts to just over ₹ 9,000 per member, emphasizing their suitability to the needs of low income families. Taken together, the rural banks record a credit-deposit ratio of 81.7 percent in March 2007, somewhat higher than the average of 76.1 percent for the entire banking system.

Rural banks have, for a number of years, been regarded as the step-child of the banking system in India. Both types of rural banks have been subject to extensive interference in their operations, being seen as a conduit for government subsidies and a means of political patronage. It is not surprising, therefore, that both the cooperative credit system and RRBs have encountered serious financial difficulties and were virtually crippled in the early 1990s, needing a substantial injection of capital at that time. The performance of such banks in recent years has been somewhat better though. Thus, 85 percent of the RRBs and around 75 percent of cooperative banks are now profitable on a year-on-year basis. While all the RRBs taken together now regularly register a profit, the DCCB performance is erratic with significant numbers slipping into losses before recovering from one year to the next. In March 2003, as many as 144 out of 367 DCBs were reported to have completely eroded their net worth and to have eroded ₹ 3,100 crore worth of deposits as well.

Importance of Rural Banks in India

Reforms to the Indian financial sector over the past 15 years have resulted in significant growth and availability of financial services. These have unleashed increased competition, diversification of financial services and wider capital markets enabled by regulatory liberalisation along with more stringent prudential regulation and better supervision. Yet substantial proportions of the population continue to be deprived of financial services. As Figure 1 shows, the Rural Financial Access Survey (RFAS) of the World Bank in 2003 found that 59 percent of rural households in Uttar Pradesh and Andhra Pradesh do not have deposit or savings accounts with the formal financial sector and 79 percent do not have access to credit from a formal source. As a separate group, 87 percent of marginal farmers and 70 percent of small farmers have no formal credit while 70 percent of marginal farmers and 45 percent of small farmers do not have deposit or savings accounts with a formal financial institution.

Credit Deployment by RRBs to Agriculture Sector

RRBs issued loans to the extent of ₹ 83,562 crore during 2010, out of which the share agriculture sector was 54.5 percent. As at end-March 2010, the outstanding advances of RRBs were ₹ 6210 crore, which accounted for only 47 percent. (Table 12.2). The share of agricultural loans increased to 54.8 Percent at end-March 2010 from 47.10 percent at end-March 2000, while the share of non-agricultural loans declined to 46.0 percent from 49.2 percent during the period.

Relative Contribution of Rural Banks to Inclusive Financial Services

Despite the apparent importance of commercial banks even in the rural areas however they are neither able nor willing to serve the poorest sections of the population. Along with their 16.2 percent contribution to the number of branches, RRBs hold just 15.7 percent of the 85.4 million loan accounts held with the banking system in the country (excluding the cooperative sector). However, in the credit categories of direct relevance to financial inclusion RRBs hold 26.2 percent of agricultural credit accounts and as many as 55.0 percent of all artisan/tiny industry loan accounts. This mounts to much lower proportions of overall credit available under these categories– just 10.9 percent and 11.0 percent respectively–since RRB loan sizes average just ₹ 25,000 and ₹ 13,000 for these two categories, much smaller than those offered by the commercial banks. Yet, it is precisely this fact that shows the importance of the rural banks for otherwise financially excluded sections of the population. Low income families have a much lower absolute and proportionate need for credit than better off sections of the population that are, in any case, better able to access the commercial banks; a factor that is important, and not often recognized.

Table 12.2: Credit Deployment by RRBs and Share of Agriculture (₹ in crore)

Year	Agriculture	Non-Agriculture	Total
2000	6210 (47.10)	6974 (52.16)	13184 (100)
2001	7250 (45.84)	8567 (54.16)	15817 (100)
2002	8405 (45.12)	10224 (54.88)	18629 (100)
2003	10261 (46.31)	11897 (53.69)	22156 (100)
2004	12320 (47.18)	13794 (52.82)	26114 (100)
2005	16710 (50.8)	16161 (49.2)	32871 (100)
2006	21394 (54.0)	18319 (46.0)	39713 (100)
2007	27,452 (56.6)	21,041 (43.4)	48,493(100)
2008	33,112 (55.4)	26,639 (44.6)	59,751(100)
2009	37,367 (55.1)	30,435 (44.8)	67,802(100)
2010	45,829 (54.8)	37,733 (45.1)	83,562(100)

Source: RBI bulletins.

Recent Developments in RRBs

In view of their proximity to rural people and better scope for understanding local conditions, RRBs are better placed to undertake micro finance operations on a large scale than are commercial banks. Since 2002, RRBs have registered a remarkable improvement in their functioning primarily as a result of their linkage with self-help groups. This linkage has not only helped them to improve their balance sheet but also enabled them to revert to their original mandate of serving the poorer sections of the rural population.

The performance of RRBs has improved significantly in terms of a number of criteria. Over a period of three years (2002-05), aggregate reserves of RRBs have increased by 124 percent while deposits and investments have increased by 39.5 percent and 20.1 percent respectively. During the same period, outstanding loans and advances increased by 76.4 percent, while loans issued increased by 99.5 percent. More important, during 1995 to 2004, their priority sector agricultural lending grew by 19.9 percent per annum and non-agricultural lending by 14.9 percent per annum. The number of profit making RRBs gradually increased from 147 in 1999 to 166 by 2005 and those reporting losses declined from 49 to 30. Moreover, the share of non-performing assets declined considerably from 27.8 percent in 1999 to 8.5 percent by 2005. But there are regional differences. In particular, NPAs of the north-eastern region (16.3 percent) continue to be very high.

Despite their better performance, RRBs have not so far been able to show a worthwhile improvement in financial margins, costs of operation and gross margins. In order to improve their financial performance, the RRBs will have to diversify their investments from low yielding government bonds to more remunerative areas. The government has taken a policy decision to strengthen RRBs by consolidating them. Consequently, the number of RRBs has been brought down from 196 in 2005 to 95 in March 2007. It has also been decided to expand the rural branch network through the RRBs. In order to improve further the functioning of the RRBs, it is important to strengthen their association with SHG linked microfinance institutions.

Re-capitalisation of RRBs

The Government of India had constituted a Committee in September 2009 (Chairman: Dr. K. C. Chakrabarty) to study the current level of Capital-to-Risk-Weighted Assets Ratio (CRAR) of RRBs and to suggest a roadmap for achieving a CRAR of 9 percent by March 2012.

The Committee was also required to suggest the required capital structure for RRBs given their business level, so that their CRAR is sustainable and provides for future growth and compliance with regulatory requirements. The Committee submitted its Report to the Government of India on April 30, 2010.

Committee on Recapitalisation of RRBs

The following are the main recommendations of the Committee on recapitalisation of RRBs.

1. The Committee carried out an assessment of capital requirement for all 82 RRBs to enable them to have CRAR of at least 7 percent as on March 31, 2011 and at least 9 percent from March 31, 2012 onwards. The recapitalisation requirement would be ₹ 2,200 crore for 40 out of the 82 RRBs. This amount may be released in two instalments, i.e., ₹ 1,338 crore in 2010-11 and ₹ 863 crore in 2011-12. The remaining 42 RRBs will not require any capital and will be able to maintain CRAR of at least 9 percent as on March 31, 2012 and thereafter on their own.
2. The Committee noted that some of the weak RRBs, particularly those in the North Eastern and Eastern regions, might not be able to fully meet all the projected business parameters despite generally achieving acceptable growth. The Committee, therefore, suggests that an additional amount of ₹ 700 crore may be kept to meet such contingencies and need based additional capitalisation provided to such RRBs once their draft balance sheets are prepared.
3. The recapitalisation of ₹ 2,200 crore to 40 RRBs should be a one-time measure, and released subject to signing of Memorandum of Understanding (MoU) by the Chairman of the RRB and on achieving the performance parameters

specified in the MoU.

4. As per Section 5 of the RRB Act, the authorized capital of RRB is ₹ 5 crore. As a result, recapitalisation amounts are kept as share capital deposit. The Committee has recommended that the accumulated losses as on March 31, 2010 may be written off against the available share capital deposits, and the balance amount of share capital deposit may be appropriated as paid-up capital. Further, in view of the expanding business of the RRBs, the Committee recommended to increase in the authorised capital of RRBs to ₹ 500 crore.
5. In order to build public confidence, in due course, RRBs with higher net worth may be allowed to access capital from the market.
6. For improving the functioning of the RRB, change of sponsor banks may be considered, wherever required.
7. RRBs with a net worth of ₹ 100 crore or more as on March 2009 may be permitted to pay dividend from April 1, 2013 onwards. RRBs to be recapitalised in the current phase may be allowed to pay dividend only after achieving a sustainable CRAR of at least 9 percent.
8. RBI may prescribe 'fit and proper' criteria for the Chairmen of RRBs. The Sponsor Bank may depute officers conforming to such criteria as Chairman on a tenure basis and wherever needed, such officers may be recruited by them from open market and then deputed to the RRBs. The compensation of Chairman may be de-linked from existing salary structure of commercial banks and be more market-oriented and a system of incentives and disincentives linked to performance benchmarks approved by the Board may be built in the compensation package.
9. The Board as a body as well as individual Board members may be made accountable for the bank's performance and individual Board members need to be assigned specific responsibilities as per their expertise.

10. Wherever required, sponsor banks may recruit suitable persons from the market, including staff of the RRBs in their own service and then depute them as General Managers in RRBs.
11. RRBs may constitute Audit Committee of the Board and conduct of Concurrent Audit and Management Audit in RRBs may be encouraged.
12. A fund of ₹ 100 crore may be set up for training and capacity building of the RRB staff.
13. The Governments, both Central and State, may include RRBs for keeping their deposits under various schemes.
14. Performance of RRBs may be monitored at National and State levels on half-yearly basis. The Sponsor Bank and NABARD may review the performance on quarterly basis. The Board of RRB will review the performance on regular basis.

Reasons for the Poor Performance of RRBs

RRBs have been relatively successful at mobilizing deposits but much less so at enhancing the credit flow to the rural poor–at least not in a professional manner. If the poor governance and financial weakness of the cooperative credit system turned it into the subject of official patronage, it was their proximity to the rural poor (not much less than that of the cooperatives), combined with government ownership that turned the RRBs into an instrument for extending subsidized credit to large numbers of people. As a result, in the words of the latest RBI working group on the RRBs, since their inception, the financial health of the RRBs has been indifferent.

According to the RBI working group, the key factors that had an effect on their performance were:

1. Limited area of operation with a narrow range of business activities and small base of clients leading to high covariant risk.
2. Focus on small customers such as small and marginal farmers, small transport operators, small and micro-

enterprises and self-help groups with limited credit requirements making it impossible to earn bulk incomes from larger, high income borrowers to cross-subsidise lending to the main customer group.

3. Perception as an instrument of social policy without viability considerations with pressure to improve financial performance, resulted in uneven growth.
4. A capital base that is too low for their business volume resulting in a serious prudential hazard whereby hundreds of crore rupees of deposits were underpinned by just ₹ 1 crore of capital. Even on 31 March 2004, 26 RRBs had a deposit base in excess of ₹ 500 crore and as many as 172 of the 196 RRBs had deposits in excess of ₹ 100 crore. This low capital base has deprived banks of the cushion normally provided by promoters' capital and has been directly responsible for the magnitude of erosion of depositor funds with 39 out of 96 banks extant on 31 March 2007 together reporting accumulated losses in excess of ₹ 2,700 crore.
5. Small organizational structure and limited financial assets come in the way of garnering a larger share of the rural financial market by making it difficult to provide a full range of financial services, thereby discouraging large depositors and borrowers.
6. High loan delinquencies resulting from their use for directed lending by the State.
7. High cost of servicing numerous small accounts while the interest cost of funds from NABARD and sponsor banks was higher than market rates but rates of interest charged to customers had to be kept in line with the competing commercial banks.
8. Poor financial skills resulting in an inefficient allocation of resources and parking of large amounts with sponsor banks.
9. Conflict of business interests with sponsor banks that operate in the same areas but have been responsible for the

financial and business initiatives of their RRBs.

10. Lack of professionalism in management as senior managers (including Chairman) are appointed out of the serving officers of the sponsor bank which results often in the reference of small matters to the sponsor with consequential delays in decision making. [It also results in short terms for Chairmen, and the notion that the job is a 'punishment' to be borne for the minimum period possible before 'coming home to the parent bank'].
11. Lack of skilled staff resulting from inappropriate training and lack of exposure to new products and development activities for catering to the changing requirements of the rural sector. An ageing staff profile resulting from the ban on recruitments has constrained efficiency in operations and uniform norms and policies across the country ignoring local issues and conditions have lowered staff morale reducing involvement in development tasks.
12. Inappropriate wage structure which was brought in line with the higher wages of the commercial banks even as RRBs were required to retain their rural flavour to identify with the rural population, yet they were required to adhere to an
13. Administered interest rate regime that depressed rates since they were lending to the "weaker sections" and yet were required to pay a slightly higher rate than commercial banks on deposits.
14. It is not surprising that by 1991, the RRBs as a banking network were on the verge of collapse with 172 of the 196 RRBs recorded as unprofitable in 1993 and a recovery performance of just 40.8 percent with a consequent erosion of public deposits in addition to the meagre ₹ 25 lakh of paid up capital.

Amalgamation of RRBs

The Advisory Committee on Flow of Credit to Agriculture and Related Activities (Chairman: Prof. V.S. Vyas) in June

2004 recommended restructuring of RRBs in order to improve the operational viability of RRBs and take advantage of the economies of scale. Following this, an Internal Working Group on RRBs was set up by the Reserve Bank to examine various alternatives available within the existing legal framework for strengthening the RRBs. In order to reposition RRBs as an effective instrument of credit delivery in the Indian financial system, the Government of India, after consultation with Nabard, the concerned State Governments and the sponsor banks initiated State-level sponsor bank-wise amalgamation of RRBs in September 2005 to overcome the deficiencies prevailing in RRBs and making them viable and profitable units.

The structural consolidation of RRBs has resulted in the formation of new RRBs, which are financially stronger and bigger in size in terms of business volume and outreach, which will enable them to take advantages of the economies of scale and reduce their operational costs. With the advantage of local feel and familiarity, RRBs are in a better position to achieve the objectives of rural development and financial inclusion. With a view to making RRBs important vehicles of credit delivery in rural and backward areas, the Reserve Bank has been taking measures from time to time for strengthening them and improving their performance. Considering the critical role of sponsor banks in positioning the RRBs as partners in the development of the rural sector and in order to encourage synergies between the parent bank and RRBs, the Reserve Bank advised all sponsor banks to take steps on issues pertaining to human resources (HR), information technology (IT) and operations of the RRBs sponsored by them.

In spite of advances in information and communication technology and considerable improvement in the institutions of decentralised governance, bureaucratic dealings persist in the form of complex land mortgage procedures. Considerable amount of paperwork, requirement of multiple visits to the banks and bribes are other existing problems. As a result, farmers incur considerable transaction costs in obtaining bank loans. This state of affairs appears to be partly because of lack of effective enforcement of directives to the scheduled commercial banks and RRBs in simplifying procedures. In the context where banks are expected to play the role of providing credit counselling to the farming community, simplifying procedures and transparency in providing credit need special attention.

Government Initiatives to Strengthen RRBs

1. A Committee constituted by the Government of India (Chairman: Dr. K.C. Chakrabarty) to examine the financials of the RRBs and suggest a roadmap to bring the CRAR of RRBs to 9 percent by March 2012 has recommended recapitalisation requirement of ₹ 2,200 crore for 40 of the 82 RRBs. The Committee has also recommended, inter alia, increase in the authorized capital of RRBs, allowing RRBs with higher net worth to access capital market in due course, improving governance, management structure and efficiency of RRBs. The recommendations of the Committee are under examination.
2. In order to strengthen and consolidate RRBs, the Government of India in 2005 initiated the process of amalgamation of RRBs in a phased manner. Consequently, the total number of RRBs has reduced from 196 to 82 as on March 31, 2010.
3. As per the status reports received from sponsor banks, 21 RRBs have migrated fully to core banking solutions (CBS) and implementation of CBS is in progress in the remaining RRBs.
4. 60 RRBs have been allowed to issue interbank participation certificates (IBPC) of a tenor of 180 days on risk-sharing basis to SCBs against their priority sector advances in excess of 60 percent of their outstanding advances.

Conclusions and Suggestions

Regional Rural Banks are playing very effective role in agricultural credit. RRBs granting loans to agricultural sector more than 50 percent of their total advances. But in recent years RRBs profits have decreased considerably. 156 RRBs were recapitalised in 2001 with ₹ 2188.44 crore and proposed to recapitalize the 2200 crore 40 RRBs out of 82 RRBs in the year 2012. Many committees have been appointed for suggesting measures for strengthening the RRBs. Presently, in our country RRBs are having operations in 535 districts with network of 15475 branches. The numbers of RRBs have been brought down to 82 from 196 through consolidation by merger of the RRBs with their sponsoring banks for improving their performance in rural areas. The major factors, which contributed to the erosion of RRBs' margins and high operating costs involved in handling of small loans. They did not have any scope of cross subsidization in the absence of loans that could yield higher returns. Wilful defaults, misuse of loans, lack of follow-up, wrong identification of borrowers, extension of benami loans, staff agitations etc. also led to poor recoveries in RRBs. The issues relating to the RRBs have been deliberated upon in the past by various Committees/Working Groups. The financial health of RRBs has been indifferent from their inception. This is caused by factors such as limited area of operation, narrow client base, high cost of servicing numerous small accounts, poor human resources of RRBs and their ineffective boards.

Following suggestions can be made for improving the performance of RRBs:

1. RRBs must rationalize and amend their loan policies and procedures so as to function as a development banker for the rural poor. RRBs must work in close coordination with the cooperative banks and rural branches of commercial banks to fill the credit gap in rural areas without any clash of mutual interests.
2. While discharging their functions as purveyors of rural

credit and mobilisers of rural savings, RRBs should not ignore the importance of financial viability and operational efficiency. The productivity, profitability and solvency of the RRBs must be maintained and sustained to enable them to function as an effective and efficient institution of rural credit.

3. Mandate of RRBs has to continue, even as they need to be restructured into viable financial institutions, simultaneously retaining their regional character and rural focus.
4. Rural bank to examine the ways of restructuring and reorganizing the productive activities of small borrowers so as to bring them to the level of generating surpluses for the purpose of reinvestment. A certain degree of flexibility of operation may be permitted with exemption in existing banking laws and regulations.
5. The qualitative and quantitative dimensions of the credit gap are so large that neither the commercial banks nor cooperative would be able to fill them up. RRBs are needed to made good some of the inadequacies in the existing rural credit system and they should become an integral part of rural credit structure.
6. The problem of the RRBs is one of improving their viability without sacrificing the basic objective for which they were set up. To impart viability to the operations of RRBs, they should be permitted to engage in all type of banking business and should not be forced to restrict their operations.
7. Banking system should be in a position to build a credit culture and discipline by equipping itself to identify the eligible clients, based on the prescribed norms, in the government sponsored schemes so that full responsibility for all aspects of credit decision remains with it. This would also help improve the client-bank relationship instead of the present system of virtually imposed clientele.

References

Gourav Vallabh and Suraj Chatrath (2006), "*Role of Banks in Agriculture and Rural Development*" The Chartered Accountant, February 2006.

M-CRIL "India's Rural Banks on the Route to Financial Inclusion" Review of Rural Banking in India: Working Paper 1, *Micro-Credit Ratings International Limited,* Gurgaon, India.

Neeraj Shrma (2010), "Role of Regional Rural Bank in Poverty Alleviation" http://www.bukisa.com, December 22nd, 2010.

R. RadhaKrishna. *"Report of Expert Group on Agricultural Indebtedness"*. Ministry of Finance, Government of India, July 2007.

Reserve Bank of India "Annual Report" RBI, Various Years.

Sukanya Bose. *"Regional Rural Banks: The Past and the Present Debate"*. www.macroscan.com/fet/jul05/pdf/RRB_Debate.pdf.

Vyas Committee. *"Advisory Committee on Flow of Credit to Agriculture and Related Activities from the Banking System"*. 2004.

Index

Index